MORAL PROGRESS

SUNY series in Philosophy
George R. Lucas, Jr., editor

MORAL PROGRESS

A Process Critique
of MacIntyre

Lisa Bellantoni

STATE UNIVERSITY OF NEW YORK PRESS

Published by
State University of New York Press, Albany

© 2000 State University of New York

Printed in the United States of America

For information, address State University of New York Press,
State University Plaza, Albany, N.Y., 12246

Production by Cathleen Collins
Marketing by Anne M. Valentine

Library of Congress Cataloging in Publication Data

Bellantoni, Lisa, 1969–
    Moral progress : a process critique of MacIntyre / Lisa
Bellantoni.
        p.   cm. — (SUNY series in philosophy)
    Includes bibliographical references and index.
    ISBN 0-7914-4443-0 (alk. paper). — ISBN 0-7914-4444-9 (pbk. :
alk. paper)
    1. MacIntyre, Alasdair C. 2. Process philosophy. 3. Ethics.
I. Title. II. Series.
B1647.M124B45 2000
170'.92—dc21   99-30969
                                                                          CIP

10 9 8 7 6 5 4 3 2 1

For Sherlock,
Love always

Contents

Abbreviations

Acknowledgments

This book simply could not have been completed without the help of several extraordinary individuals with whom I have had the privilege to associate. My thanks go first to the following members of the Philosophy Department at Vanderbilt University: John Lachs, for helping me to see this project through from beginning to end, in ways equally innumerable and invaluable, and for doing so with his characteristic kindness and generosity; Henry Teloh, for getting me into this mess in the first place, and for helping me to see my way out, such as it is; John Compton and Jeffrey Tlumak, for asking all the right questions, at just the right times; and finally, to the department as a whole, faculty, students, and staff members, for helping me to make my time there so rewarding. Among these fine people I wish to mention in particular Pat Shade, now of Rhodes College, and Christie Allen, for so forthrightly showing me the errors of my ways. Most importantly, my thanks go to my favorite overgrown leprechaun, James F. Sheridan of Allegheny College, whose assistance quite literally made this book possible, who taught me everything I know and then some, and for whom no words can express my appreciation, my respect, my affection, and my gratitude.

The following publishers have generously granted permission from copyrighted works:

From *After Virtue: A Study in Moral Theory*, Second Edition by Alasdair MacIntyre. © 1984 by Alasdair MacIntyre and by University of Notre Dame Press. Used by permission of the publisher.

From *Whose Justice? Which Rationality?* by Alasdair MacIntyre. © 1988 by Alasdair MacIntyre and by University of Notre Dame Press. Used by permission of the publisher.

Introduction

A lasdair MacIntyre's influential work, *After Virtue*, presents readers a stark choice: revive our traditional moral practices in toto, or surrender any pretense to them. For MacIntyre, viable traditions of moral discourse and enquiry effect among their adherents univocal rational agreement both upon the ends a good life embodies and the appropriate means to pursue them. Absent such consensus, as our contemporary practical disputes make evident, moral discourse sinks into insoluable disagreements; indeed, MacIntyre's diagnosis has itself spawned numerous debates. Yet that result illustrates his central point. Awash as we are in an emotivist culture, wherein practical disputes are widely believed to assay personal preferences alone, our competing practical claims inevitably prove rationally incommensurable.

According to MacIntyre, the "interminable" moral disputes we face signal the ascent of emotivism, the belief "that all evaluative judgments and more specifically all moral judgments are nothing but expressions of preference, expressions of attitude or feeling" (AV:11). This view infects our moral discourse—covertly. Underlying this discourse lurks a conceptual schizophrenia: we still use traditional moral terms—justice and virtue, for example—despite having abandoned the shared beliefs and practices that once gave them univocal moral content. For that reason these terms no longer function as they once did, as objective evaluative standards. Instead they mask the rational incommensurability of current moral controversies, whose participants, now lacking that common linguistic and normative framework, largely speak past one another.

This conceptual disarray arises from two Enlightenment legacies: the rejection first of traditional social beliefs and practices as a source of moral normativity, and second of any teleological understanding of

1

human life. In cutting moral standards adrift from their traditional moorings, MacIntyre argues, Enlightenment theorists left their successors two irresolvable problems. First, in denying the teleological link between human nature and our practical ideals, they denied the operative ideal that had once animated the practical enterprise, the belief that moral practice aims at human perfectability. Second, in abstracting those ideals from the practices and beliefs that formerly limned that perfectability, they precluded those ideals from serving as bases for objective evaluative judgments.

Such judgments, MacIntyre argues, presuppose substantive agreement both upon the ends we properly seek and the means by which we might pursue them, such that practical disputes are in principle resolvable. Yet emotivism, deferring to individual preferences as the final arbiter of appropriate means and ends, undercuts such a framework. This result, however, signals not that emotivism is inescapable but that Enlightenment efforts to reject tradition-constituted and teleological modes of practical reasoning were deeply mistaken. Indeed, MacIntyre contends, if we accept the emotivist recourse we abandon not only traditional moral claims but the very possibility of practical enquiry: "I am not merely contending that morality is not what it once was, but also and more importantly that what was once morality has to some large degree disappeared—and that this marks a degeneration, a grave cultural loss" (AV:21).

Animating MacIntyre's rejection of emotivism is his understanding of moral enquiry as irremediably rooted in a particular tradition's practices. In apprenticing themselves to a moral tradition, MacIntyre argues, enquirers reenact the tradition's distinctive narrative, through which they come to grasp how that tradition's standards acquire their intelligibility, justification, and motivational force. Indeed, for MacIntyre normative standards acquire their rational authority through this recapitulation. Practical rationality inhabits a tradition, such that enquiry within that tradition must conform its progress to the standards by which, for example, that tradition ranks and integrates human goods. Lacking such conformity, MacIntyre argues, practical enquiry could not include rational debate, because no reasons could be given for pursuing some practices or modes of life rather than others.

Yet those assessments are precisely the judgments that not only emotivist but also Enlightenment and Enlightenment-inspired theorists cannot make. For MacIntyre practical reasoning is both substantive and particularist; its operative claims are bound for their intelligibility, justification, and motive force to the tradition it inhabits. Accordingly contemporary efforts to uncover the universal conditions of moral discourse and practice, like those of their Enlightenment predecessors, cannot succeed in securing universal assent and conflict resolution. According to such theories, practical reason is procedural rather than substantive, such that practical principles must be justified apart from reference to any particular tradition. Yet as MacIntyre rightly argues, these proceduralist accounts have never succeeded even in showing that practical reason admits such universal conditions, much less in securing universal assent for a specific set of such conditions. If anything, he suggests, these efforts' manifest failures stoke the emotivism that these accounts must also reject.

While universalist efforts may inevitably fail to secure consensus, MacIntyre's account of practical reason exhibits a similar problem, a problem originating in his insular conception of practical traditions. On MacIntyre's view, practical enquiry requires one's initiation into a particular tradition, so much so that to engage a tradition apart from one's own requires one's learning what he terms a "second first language." This account implies that practical rationality is tradition constituted, such that traditions are rationally incommensurable and conceptually isolated from one another. Yet as MacIntyre's analyses suggest, no enduring tradition has proved thus isolated, either in its founding or in its perpetuation. To cite even his examples, the Thomist tradition he avows borrowed readily from its Aristotelean predecessors, belying the claim that one tradition's conceptual content is incommunicable to rival traditions.

Moreover, while contemporary disputes may prove interminable, so too do many debates marking the traditions MacIntyre avers. The Thomist virtue of humility, for example, is deeply at odds with the Aristotelean virtue of proper pride. That virtues become vices and vices virtues is not uncommon in the history of such traditions' interchanges. Yet that pattern suggests not that virtue traditions are wholly incommensurable rivals, their resources incommunicable, but that they confront similar problems and draw upon a common well of practical and theoretical options to resolve them. To that extent, MacIntyre's claim that functional traditions are closed systems wherein disputes are in principle rationally resolvable oversimplifies the function of practical reason. Indisputably, viable traditions afford their members common languages and reasoning patterns by which to resolve their disputes. Yet in that process such traditions' practical concerns inevitably evolve, expanding beyond the range of their current resources to resolve.

To take another of MacIntyre's examples, in his lengthy discussion of justice he documents the confusion this term has engendered following upon Enlightenment efforts to secularize it. Those modern debates, however, are no more incommensurable than are those marking the premodern traditions he avows. For Aristotle, for instance, justice required treating equals equally, equals including citizens alone. For Aquinas, justice had a similar imperative, yet it extended well beyond the polis Aristotle envisioned to include all Christians. Moreover, despite these positions' seeming incommensurability, both countenanced a partially shared ideal of justice; they disputed who qualified as an equal, not whether equals warranted equal treatment.

Such examples illustrate a threefold point. First, even those traditions arrayed around the Aristotelean and Thomist ideals MacIntyre avows are not conceptually isolated; rather, they appropriate each others' resources. Second, these traditions are themselves not fully commensurable, nor are their internal disputes fully resolvable. Third, while their developments do aim to resolve their mutual disputes, those disputes do not undermine but strengthen these traditions. As MacIntyre rightly maintains, practical enquiry perpetuates ideals. Yet these ideals remain living options precisely insofar as they are contested by and absorbed into competing traditions. To this extent practical enquiry functions not only to resolve practical disputes, but also to evoke and sustain the conflicts among basic, even incommensurable, principles that demand the creation and discovery of additional practical resources to resolve.

That dual function, of creating and discovering novel ideals, as well as of recapitulating one's tradition and its constitutive ideals, implies that MacIntyre oversimplifies the purposes of practical apprenticeship. For MacIntyre, that function is largely recapitulative, restoring a tradition's practical ideals in succeeding generations. I suggest instead that traditions' main function is to distill ideals that lure future commitments as they illuminate or resolve current challenges, and that wane when they no longer offer living possibilities. Incommensurable conflict, within and among traditions, is thus both a product and a condition of practical enquiry—not its undoing. Practical enquiry's aim, then, is not merely to secure social consensus within particular traditions, but to expand the range of living ideals available to those traditions.

Ascribing to practical reason this dual role suggests a ready alternative to MacIntyre's account of practical enquiry. As MacIntyre's own genealogies suggest, traditions are neither as insular nor as incommensurable as he maintains; nor is practical enquiry as bound to a single tradition for its enactment. Rather, traditions draw their vigor from their competiton to offer animating ideals, ends, and principles. That competition, moreover, suggests that traditions face some common practical problems and draw from and contribute to a partially shared stock of practical resources to resolve them, rendering their disputes partly commensurable. Conversely, this account of practical enquiry suggests a view of practical conflict, its conditions and prospects for resolution, better able on MacIntyre's own terms to explain and confront the emotivist challenge.

Yet if, as I will argue, MacIntyre's discussion misconceives practical traditions, distorts how practical reason functions, and to what ends, and thereby bolsters the emotivism he rightly aims to resist, why pursue a criticism of his work? For two reasons. First, while his diagnosis of the contemporary emotivist recourse is inaccurate, his account gives voice to a powerful cultural undercurrent that aims at practical univocity and moral consensus. Indeed, this undercurrent animates both his position and the positions of his Enlightenment-inspired competitors, competitors he rightly criticizes. Second, the emotivism he contests does present a powerful challenge to moral discourse and practice, undercutting those common expectations—that moral matters can be rationally assessed, disputed, and resolved, that our means of doing so are coherent, that our moral commitments express more than our individual preferences— which underlie moral practice in any proper sense of the term.

Indeed, if emotivism triumphs its consequences may well be as MacIntyre envisions them, as it would reduce our common moral intuitions, practices, and convictions to nonsense, and would contravene the entirety of that tradition from which those intuitions and practices grew. For these reasons, we must better understand both the disputes we currently face and their origins in the traditions we've inherited. More importantly, however, we must also come to recognize why we must resist both MacIntyre's account and those advanced by his Enlightenment-inspired rivals. We must resist such accounts, demanding as they do rational univocity and moral consensus as conditions of practical enquiry, because under any guise this latter insistence stokes the emotivism both efforts rightly reject.

We must resist this demand for practical univocity, I will argue, because the emotivist challenge does not emanate from the conceptual disarray our inheritances currently present us. Rather, it flows from the narrow cognitivism, shared by universalist and particularist accounts of practical enquiry, that insists that rational resolvability is the hallmark of rational debate. This requirement cannot help but bolster emotivism, as it regards conflict resolution as a condition of practical rationality, and so focuses on the justification of practical claims. Yet as MacIntyre's own genealogies suggest, the ideals, ends, and principles we inherit become subject to justificatory proof only after they have secured their initial intelligibility and motive force. Such ideals must be seen not first as rationally justified but as having proposed seductive possibilities. Practical reasoning thus coalesces around such prospects, their incipient rationality inciting agents' efforts to justify those principles vis-à-vis other practical possibilities.

To that end, narrowly cognitivist accounts of practical enquiry misconceive its function, directing it to secure practical resolutions rather than to distill enticing ideals. That cognitivism dessicates contemporary moral discourse, whose obsessive focus on determining prescriptions rather than proposing aspirations perpetuates the unproductive disputes—for example, between universalist and particularist theorists— that lend emotivist claims currency. Those disputes, however, are not unproductive because they indicate failures of rational justification, or in MacIntyre's terms, are rationally interminable. Rather, they are unproductive because they betray their participants' impoverished practical imaginations, their inability to propose novel ideals able to elicit broad-based allegiance.

To respond to the emotivist challenge, then, we must reconsider how practical traditions embody rationality and to what extent they permit dispute resolution. On both counts, I will argue, Alfred North Whitehead's metaphysical teleology offers the basis for an account of practical rationality best able to address these challenges. This account will more effectively bolster practical reason's claims than will reigning cognitivist approaches. It will do so by proposing a broader cognitivism that uncovers practical enquiry's emotive and motivational bases, and that traces how practical enquiries unfurl from those bases. Thereby, it will root the intelligibility and justification of practical claims within the emotive processes from which practical enquiry takes flight, and to which it inevitably recurs.

This broader cognitivism, positing evolving bases for practical claims' intelligibility, motive force, and justification, renders such claims commensurable and truth evaluable, denying emotivism's charges to the contrary. Yet it does so because it embraces two points both MacIntyre and his Enlightenment-inspired adverseries reject: first, that the ethical enterprise, aiming at human perfectability, is an essentially metaphysical undertaking; second, that practical enquiry aims not only to secure social consensus within traditions, but also to distill the competing ideals that drive practical life forward.

These recognitions are critical because the emotivist recourse MacIntyre excoriates is not merely at odds with our practical inheritances, but is falsified on metaphysical grounds. Practical life, a Whiteheadian account suggests, inhabits a teleology subject to two central aims: novel and intense experience. Those aims qualify the ideals practical traditions propose and the traditions that embody them. These ideals endure as they prove productive, useful, and enticing for their adherents, yet their achievements are fragile and must be reenacted and recreated. They must not only propose novel perfections, then, but must also secure adherents beyond their originating traditions, affording thereby the transtraditional ideals that render practical traditions partly commensurable.

Amid this unfolding, traditions may well prove cognates when they propose contrasting ideals. Such ideals, however, do not undermine practical rationality. Rather they evoke the rational activity requisite for any tradition to integrate or exclude those ideals as they cohere or fail to cohere with that tradition's past inheritances, present purposes, and future prospects. Practical enquiries perpetually recreate the intelligibility, motive force, and justification of the practical resources they inherit. The ideals, ends, and principles, the practical resources thus inherited, thereby prove both substantive and processive, both tied to the traditions originally spawning them, and available as practical possibilities to competing traditions. Accordingly, those resources are neither self-sustaining nor wholly enduring; rather, enquirers must recreate them if they are to preserve the practical truths they once embodied.

This account suggests an evolving ideal of practical justification, and a transtraditional account of practical intelligibility. Practical enquiry is particularist, bound as it is to its origins. Yet the ideals particular traditions propose aspire to universality, offering enduring ideals for reenactment and recreation. Such ideals permit partially commensurable discourse insofar as traditions confront common problems and draw from a shared stock of inherited ideals to resolve them. Moreover, they endure as they offer agents live options with which to address these challenges, yet dissipate as they fail to induce such reenactments and recreations.

This account implies that the incommensurable conflicts practical enquiry admits are a condition of its progress, not a signal of its decay. Interminable disputes imperil moral enquiry only on the assumption that rational disputes entail wholesale rational resolution. Yet that narrow cognitivism both distorts the history of practical enquiry and a priori renders the emotivist challenge unanswerable. That practical enquiry aims properly at social consensus, insofar as such consensus renders practical ideals socially efficacious, is undeniable. Yet those ideals endure not first through their rational defense, but through their motivational force and intelligibility, through the lures they offer for recreation. Such lures incite our practical imaginations, stoking the tripartite urge that animates the practical faith, the vision of moral progress our enquiries properly embody: the urge not only to live or to live well—but to live better.

1

The Emotivist Challenge

According to Alasdair MacIntyre, the "interminable" moral disputes we face today signal the ascendency of emotivism: "Emotivism is the doctrine that all evaluative judgments and more specifically all moral judgments are nothing but expressions of preference, expressions of attitude or feeling, insofar as they are moral or evaluative in character" (AV:11).[1] This view infects our moral discourse—covertly. Underlying this discourse lurks a conceptual schizophrenia: we still use traditional moral language despite having abandoned the social and historical contexts that once—but no longer—lent its animating terms univocal normative content. Accordingly, while words such as 'justice' and 'virtue' haunt contemporary moral discourse, they cannot function as they once did, as impersonal evaluative standards. Absent that functionality, our fragmented moral discourse leaves us unable to secure rational practical agreements.

That confusion, for example, drives our seemingly endless disputes over the appropriate principles of distributive justice. Liberals and communitarians, utility theorists and libertarians, all invoke a common terminology, while using that terminology's definitive concepts, 'justice' and 'merit,' differently. Worse still, these positions propose different normative standards while presupposing that resolving disagreements among them requires reference to shared, impersonal standards. Such standards, these cognitivist theories maintain, distinguish irresolvable disputes about preferences from moral disputes that are rationally adjudicable. MacIntyre shares this view: "The particular link between the context of utterance and the force of reason-giving which always holds in the case of expressions of personal preferences or desire is severed in the case of moral and other evaluative utterances" (AV:9).

For emotivists, however, contemporary theorists' evident failure to identify such universal normative standards indicates that that link remains: "For what emotivism asserts is in central part that there can be no valid rational justification for any claims that objective and impersonal moral standards exist and hence that there are no such standards" (AV:18). Yet that conclusion follows only from emotivists' ahistoricism. According to MacIntyre, the moral terms contemporary theorists have inherited "were originally at home in larger totalities of theory and practice in which they enjoyed a role and function supplied by contexts of which they have now been deprived" (AV:10). Emotivists lack that recognition, believing— falsely—that current moral disputes are irresolvable because all moral disputes are rationally interminable: "What I have suggested to be the case by and large about our own culture—that in moral argument the apparent assertion of principles functions as a mask for expressions of personal preference—is what emotivism takes to be universally the case" (AV:18).

Yet emotivism is neither a viable theoretical position nor an accurate depiction of moral discourse. Its apparent cogency results from a series of theoretical transitions that systematically stripped moral evaluation of its objective normative force. Accordingly he seeks both to show how emotivism gains force historically, and to restore the normative contexts from which traditional moral claims were illicitly wrested. The roots of emotivism MacIntyre locates in the Enlightenment. Enlightenment theorists largely agreed upon a set of moral precepts and the form their rational vindication would take. They proposed to justify those precepts by arguing from factual premises about human nature to the moral principles that nature implied. Their efforts failed, however, because these theorists rejected any teleological conception linking moral precepts to humans' factual nature: "All reject any teleological view of human nature, any view of man as having an essence which defines his true end" (AV:52).

Reenforcing this rejection were those theorists who claimed that moral oughts could not derive from factual premises. Such a view was fatal to the Enlightenment moral project:

> Since the whole point of ethics is to enable man to pass from his present state to his true end, the elimination of any notion of essential human nature and with it the abandonment of any notion of a telos leaves behind a moral scheme composed of two remaining elements whose relationship becomes quite unclear. (AV:52)

Moreover, the claim that moral oughts cannot be derived from factual sources evinces an elementary logical mistake.[2] That claim, MacIntyre maintains, expresses not a timeless logical truth but a consequence of overthrowing teleological modes of understanding. Such understanding underlies arguments of a particular is-ought form, those including functional concepts. These concepts define their objects, for example, watches, by reference not to their parts or operative principles but to their functions or uses. Functional concepts allow us to factually evaluate objects as good according to how well such objects work.

And in the tradition MacIntyre takes to predate our current moral confusion, "man" is a functional concept: "Within this tradition moral and evaluative statements can be called true or false in precisely the way in which all other factual statements can be so called" (AV:57). Enlightenment theorists, rushing to overthrow all teleological references, dissevered human nature and moral precepts, rendering ambiguous the latter's prescriptive relation to the former: "But once the notion of essential human purposes or functions disappears from morality, it begins to appear implausible to treat moral judgments as factual statements" (AV:57). Indeed, he suggests, unraveling that teleological linkage undercuts any possibility of factually vindicating normative claims.

MacIntyre's Alternative: The Virtue Tradition

To restore a factual vindication of normative authority, MacIntyre proposes to reconstruct a teleological ethic consonant with the Aristotelean and Thomist conceptions of moral enquiry. Thereby he aims to reinstitute a normative context affording moral claims adjudicable evaluative content. His account, he claims, links moral evaluation and the explanation of particular actions such that agents' actions are morally evaluable, as for emotivists such actions are not. That linkage underlies the Aristotelean conception of practical rationality that locates evaluative concepts such as 'justice' within a teleological cosmology. Such a cosmology supplies an arché or set of first principles delimiting the human telos:

> Those archai, if correctly formulated, will furnish us with the
> first principles for the explanation of how and why human enter-
> prises and activities are better or worse at achieving those goods

which provide them with their telos, and they will do so precisely by formulating adequately an account of those goods and their place in or relationship to the good and the best. (WJ:92)[3]

This arché, MacIntyre claims, orders human goods and their relation to the Good, specifying standards of human excllence. Agents exemplify those standards through their performance of practices:

> By a 'practice' I am going to mean any coherent and complex form of socially established cooperative human activity through which goods internal to that form of activity are realised in the course of trying to achieve those standards of excellence which are appropriate to, and partially definitive of, that form of activity, with the result that human powers to achieve excellence, and human conceptions of the ends and goods involved, are systematically extended. (AV:175)

Practices are not techniques for pursuing extrinsic goods. They exhibit a "unique regard" for their own internal goods and for the extension of human powers they permit (AV:180). That extension requires practitioners to internalize the objective standards defining mastery of the practices they pursue. MacIntyre grants that practices' standards are not immune to criticism. Nevertheless he argues, novices must accept as authoritative guides the best standards thus far achieved if they are to master and advance their practices. This necessity precludes emotivist pretentions: "In the realm of practices the authority of both goods and standards operates in such a way as to rule out all subjectivist and emotivist analyses of judgment" (AV:177).

New members master practices, MacIntyre maintains, by absorbing the impersonal standards practices uphold for evaluating participants' performances. Using chess as an analogue, MacIntyre describes how novice players internalize the objective standards defining mastery of this activity. They acquire expertise by modeling their play after that of exemplary players and by submitting themselves to requirements independent of their preferences. They do so, for example, by crediting others' evaluations of their progress, by accepting instruction, and by eliminating their weaknesses. More importantly, MacIntyre argues, novices' efforts to advance their expertise demand also that they increasingly embody the virtues—among them justice, courage, and honesty—which progressively integrate them into the broader cultural practices according such terms their widest normative force: "A virtue is an acquired human quality the possession and exercise of which tends to enable us to achieve those goods which are internal to practices and the lack of which effectively prevents us from achieving any such goods" (AV:178).

The goods practices accrue and the virtues they encourage must be contextualized to function normatively. Apart from the narrative unity of an agent's life and that life's residence in a shared telos transcending and unifying individual practices, agents could specify neither why particular activities require particular virtues, nor why some activities should be valued more than others. Virtues' normative functions, MacIntyre insists, cannot be specified apart from their inherences across an agent's life "conceived and evaluated as a whole" (AV:190–91). That integral life presupposes a narrative history causally ordering an agent's intentions and actions according to their role in the agent's history (AV:193–94). Such narratives render human actions evaluable and human agents accountable for their narratives.

For MacIntyre, moral agents are "storytellers whose stories aspire to truth" (AV:201). Agents exhibit that aspiration as they nest their narratives in a shared tradition. Just as an individual life's constancy embodies that life's moral unity, so that unity inhabits a broader view of the good life. To pursue such a life agents must engage in practices which secure internal goods, extend human powers, and develop virtues. Thereby agents assume residence in a living tradition, a historically extended social argument about the goods and virtues constituting that tradition: "The good life for man is the life spent in seeking for the good life for man, and the virtues necessary for the seeking are those which will enable us to understand what more and what else the good life for man is" (AV:204).

To that end, practical rationality conforms these deliberations to teleological standards hierarchizing and integrating human goods (WJ:131). Agents can realize the good life only when their actions aim at the intrinsic goods that practices reap and only when those activities evoke and sustain virtues. If no hierarchy of goods obtained, agents could give no reasons for pursuing some practices rather than others, nor could they accord any particular conception of the good life's requisite virtues univocal authority. To exercise such virtues, agents must understand both the hierarchy of goods the human telos specifies and their roles within that hierarchy. That localization enjoins agents to develop that telos' requisite virtues through practices which aim to realize its consonant goods, such that all agents' pursuits are oriented toward the Good (WJ:110–18).

The Enlightenment Legacy

Only when agents share a conception of the good life, MacIntyre maintains, as they did in the Aristotelean polis, can they rationally agree upon the relative merits of different activities and goods. Yet, he maintains, the contemporary liberal state—the emotivist's natural habitat—embodies a conception of practical rationality that precludes social consensus. Its interminable disagreements result inevitably from its Enlightenment inheritances. Enlightenment theorists sought to provide a political, moral, and legal framework whose neutral standards would permit disparate goods to coexist. To that end Enlightenment theorists eschewed tradition-dependent principles, instead premising their normative claims either upon moral truths evident to all rational agents, or upon procedural principles of right conduct (WJ:332):

> Initially the liberal claim was to provide a political, legal, and economic framework in which assent to one and the same set of rationally justifiable principles would enable those who espouse widely different and incompatible conceptions of the good life for human beings to live together peaceably within the same society, enjoying the same political status and engaging in the same economic relationships. (WJ:335–36)

Their varigated efforts, however, specified the intuitions and facts underlying those principles differently, precluding neutral factual appeals to resolve competing claims. Additionally, the contending positions offered neither an uncontested account of what criteria a tradition-independent morality should satisfy, nor any neutral criteria for adjudicating those claims. Moreover, their project's aim was from the start not neutral, as it required heteronomous goods to coexist, forbidding any conception of practical rationality which sought to advance a single, overriding Good:

> Every individual is to be equally free to propose and to live by whatever conception of the good he or she pleases . . . unless that conception of the good involves reshaping the life of the rest of the community in accordance with it. Any conception of the human good according to which, for example, it is the duty of government to educate the members of the community morally, so that they come to live out that conception of the good . . . will be proscribed. (WJ:336)

Such a political and cultural order makes individuals' pursuit of disparate interests and preferences its highest good. Accordingly, the normative principles it offers will not socially order human goods but will encourage agents to pursue their individual preferences. Moreover, as it will commend no hierarchy of preferences, agents will have no reasons for ordering their preferences in one way rather than another:

> The heterogeneity is such that no overall ordering of goods is possible. And to be educated into the culture of a liberal social order is, therefore, characteristically to become the kind of person to whom it appears normal that a variety of goods should be pursued, each appropriate to its own sphere, with no overall good supplying any overall unity to life. (WJ:337)

On this view, MacIntyre claims, practical reasoning allows agents not to evaluate their preferences but merely to translate them into decisions and actions aimed at satisfying individual wants. That process debases moral discourse and practice because it permits no rational resolution among preferred activities and ends. As no univocal hierarchy of preferences obtains, agents cannot identify true normative premises, thus cannot rationally resolve their disputes. Such social orders render moral discourse merely rhetorical, expressing not agents' impersonal, rational judgments but individuals' attitudes, feelings, and choices.

Within this context contemporary agents can neither evaluate moral situations nor render their own or others' activities intelligible. The premodern agent has its moral life constituted for it by its roles, obligations, and practices. These social strictures afford both a shared teleology and the impersonal standards by which that agent can evaluate human practices and goods. In contrast:

> The specifically modern self, the self that I have called emotivist, finds no limits set to that on which it may pass judgment for such limits could only derive from rational criteria for evaluation and, as we have seen, the emotivist self lacks any such criteria. Everything may be criticized from whatever standpoint the self has adopted, including the self's choice of standpoint to adopt. (AV:30)

Modern theorists no longer tie moral agency essentially to the roles, obligations, and practices one assumes: "Anyone and everyone can thus be a moral agent, since it is in the self and not in social roles or practices that moral agency has to be located" (AV:30). This account liberates the modern agent from traditional social bonds. Yet it does so at a price:

> But from this it follows that the emotivist self can have no rational history in its transitions from one state of moral commitment to another. Inner conflicts are for it necessarily au fond the confrontation of one contingent arbitrariness by another. (AV:30–31)

The Thomist Synthesis

According to MacIntyre, Enlightenment theorists maintained that rational debate, adequately conducted, embodied universal normative standards any rational person would assent to. Such assent would eliminate moral judgments' reference to traditional authorities. Practical progress, these theorists maintained, required liberating agents from the irrational prohibitions of the moral traditions they had inherited. That task was best served by presenting practical rationality not as historically embodied but as a function of universally evident procedural principles (TRV:172–77).[4]

Their failure to univocally justify any such principles, however, engendered the familiar attacks launched against Enlightenment moralists by Nietzsche and his genealogical progeny. For Nietzsche the fate of the Enlightenment moralists was the fate of all moralists: their truth claims were riddled with unrecognized motives serving unacknowledged purposes. There is, Nietzsche insisted, no moral truth and no moral progress. Rather, such concepts mask the moralists' will-to-truth, a will inseparable from their will-to-power. These themes, developed by Nietzsche's successors, such as Foucault, depicted moral orders not as unfolding rational traditions but as confluences of power aiming to preserve their hegemony (TRV:53).

Yet even if these genealogical analyses accurately depict Enlightenment theorists' legacy, MacIntyre claims, their methods have serious flaws. Nietzsche's perspectivism, maintaining that practical claims embody truth only from their animating perspectives, should deny its own truth claims as it does those of competing perspectives (TRV:35–42). Moreover, lacking such a shared theoretical context, Nietzsche like Foucault can have no audience (TRV:55–57). More importantly, their methods fatally misunderstand how narrative functions in constructing practical rationality. The genealogists claim that their analyses betray a succession not of rational traditions but of wills-to-power. Modern moralities might exhibit such disarray, MacIntyre grants. But they do so because they reject the premodern traditions that alone sustain a shared conception of the human good, depriving agents of any intelligible context amid which to locate normative claims (TRV:193–95).

His genealogical rivals, MacIntyre claims, contrast their conception of practical rationalities as representing masked power interests with the Enlightenment's view of practical rationality as a universal, proceduralist enterprise. Yet that contrast omits the Thomist conception of practical enquiry qua craft. On this account enquirers fulfill practical enquiry's telos by apprenticing themselves to its masters and cultivating the virtues such enquiry embodies. In thus apprenticing oneself one opposes both the Enlightenment injunction to think for oneself and the genealogical suspicion of authority. Instead, one reenacts practical enquiry's history to understand how its standards come to secure legitimate authority. According to MacIntyre, Aguinas exemplifies this conduct of moral enquiry as historical narrative. By drawing upon Aquinas' example, he suggests, we can come to recognize how the Thomist conception of moral enquiry is superior to its contemporary competitors (TRV:79–81).

Aguinas' central task, MacIntyre maintains, was to merge the Aristotelean and Augustinian traditions he inherited. From Augustine he took over a theistic moral psychology depicting God as the source of all practical intelligibility. While proper instruction can orient human minds toward that intelligibility and the timeless normative standards it embodies, the human will is a perverse and countervailing force. As those standards are available only to those whose minds are illumined by God, faith in authority precedes rational understanding, which is attainable only through divine grace (TRV:84). For Aristotle, in contrast, human intelligence is adequate to the objects of practical rationality. Accordingly, Aristotle affirms both practical reason's independence of theology and the identity of virtue with natural rather than revealed knowledge.

Aquinas faced the challenge of integrating these accounts despite their different standards of rationality and their distinct theoretical and practical aims (TRV:101–16). To resolve these positions, MacIntyre maintains, Aquinas referred them jointly toward the common reality to which they pointed, the metaphysical ground that Augustine's and Aristotle's accounts shared. That ground, MacIntyre maintains, was best characterized as 'God,' the theological mechanism even Aristotle's cosmology called for as its underlying principle of unity. Positing such a ground as the foundation of his enquiry supplied Aquinas a common framework that permitted his Aristotelean and Augustinian inheritances to complement each other, rendering their common objects more intelligible (TRV:123–26).

This approach, MacIntyre maintains, affirms Aquinas' treatment of practical enquiry as a craft and his commitment to that craft's tradition and its archai. Aquinas recognized that these traditions were by themselves metaphysically and theologically inadequate, and sought to preserve the strengths of both by constructing a more inclusive and coherent position integrating their essential intuitions. To that end he affirms with Aristotle that humans are rational animals, yet affirms with Augustine that such creatures are afflicted with perverse wills. He then articulates a mode of life wherein knowledge of God is necessary to fully apprehend the Good, and wherein one must evince faith and virtue before understanding one's commitments to that life.

In merging these traditions, Aquinas aimed to identify and advance the excellences previous enquiries had achieved, as would the exemplary practitioner of any well-ordered craft. Such crafts inhabit narrative traditions. Aquinas' account offers a narrative initiates must reenact if they are to understand why certain virtues are commended and why obedience to divine law serves the human good. Reenacting that narrative presupposes a particular kind of enquirer seeking to enter a particular community, presuppositions apart from which Aquinas' account cannot be understood. The initiate, then, reenacts a narrative presupposing certain truths about God, human nature, and morality amid which alone additional truths may be identified (TRV:132–37).

Those presuppositions circumscribe conceptions of truth, of rational justification, and of practical intelligibility wholly at odds with those of modern theorists. For Aristotle, Aquinas, Augustine, for the premodern tradition, moral enquiry aimed to actualize the mind's potential, to reveal how practical truths assume their necessary form (FP:14–15).[5] Such understanding, MacIntyre claims, embodies a deductive scheme hierarchically structuring its causal explanations. The best explanations yield first principles specifying causes that refer directly to a singular first cause: God. Such enquiry entails a theological referent because it aspires to unify the intelligibility, motive force, and justification of its practical claims, an intelligibility secured only by the comprehensive unity of explanation a theological system affords (FP:27–29).

The Rationality of Traditions

To advance this enquiry, its practitioners must reenact those narratives through which its practical truths and their rational justification have come to be understood (FP:30–33). Every enquiry, MacIntyre argues, progresses toward its telos as a perfected science, uncovering those determinate goods delimiting its particular mode of life. Yet modern theorists, MacIntyre maintains, thoroughly reject this conception of rational enquiry as embodied in and developed by reference to tradition. The teleological concepts such enquiry presupposes are defensible only in a universe including determinate ends by which individual purposes can be ordered. Absent such an arche, the modern moral project dissolves human agency into a heteronomous array of purposes issuing from individual interests, desires, and decisions. Lacking determinate ends, any singular hierarchy comes to be seen as invented or chosen rather than as discovered, hence as devoid of the normative authority by which it might claim to guide agents toward the fulfillment of a given telos.

Yet that lack of a determinate telos, MacIntyre claims, is not, as his genealogical rivals suggest, the universal moral situation we face. Rather it issues from the Enlightenment's misguided project. This fault line between contemporary Thomists and genealogists, signifying their disparate judgments upon the Enlightenment's abortive project, underscores how MacIntyre aims to show the Thomist position to be superior to its contemporary rivals. MacIntyre maintains that to understand an enquiry one must understand its narrative history, a narrative that can only be told in one way. Absent such a determinate accounting, no tradition could vindicate itself; indeed, it would betray inconsistencies even in self-narration. Accordingly, he suggests, the account he proposes proves superior to its contemporary rivals in part because it explains these rivals as consequences of the failed Enlightenment project, rendering the history of practical enquiry more intelligible than do these rival accounts (FP:48–51).

The Enlightenment legacy, MacIntyre maintains, culminates in the emotivist view that no tradition is rationally superior to any other, dooming individuals to the relativism and perspectivism that emotivism portends. According to the relativist, the logical incompatability and incommensurability of practical claims reign across competing traditions, undercutting agents' ability to choose rationally among them "if the only available standards of rationality are those made available by and within traditions, then no issue between contending traditions is rationally decidable" (WJ:352). The perspectivist, seeing competing traditions not as logically incompatible but as complementary, denies the possibility of particular traditions harboring true claims:

> [T]he perspectivist challenge puts in question the possibility of making truth claims from within any one tradition. For if there is a multiplicity of rival traditions . . . that very fact entails that no one tradition can offer those outside it good reasons for excluding the theses of its rivals. Yet if this is so . . . no one tradition can deny legitimacy to its rivals. (WJ:352)

Yet both positions, he maintains, fail to recognize the rationality of traditions. The rationality implicit in practical enquiry, MacIntyre claims, develops through four stages. Enquirers begin by accepting their tradition's beliefs, institutions, and practices. That acceptance confers authority upon certain voices and texts. Those texts and voices, however, inevitably confront questions raised by novel interpretations, internal incoherencies, and new social challenges. To address such challenges, the tradition's adherents reformulate the framework either by using its internal resources, or by inventing novel resources, or by borrowing resources from rival traditions.

Practical traditions thereby develop and test their adequacy dialectically, moving toward a coherence whose successive claims more closely approximate a final, adequate position. Such traditions counter the dissolution of their historical certitudes by inventing or discovering or borrowing concepts and principles that systematically and coherently explain why the tradition's previous claims proved inadequate and how they may be improved. These enquiries thereby delimit that tradition's historically warranted assertability standards; standards, however, which are invariably conditioned by the mind's adequation to its objects (WJ:357–64):

> The concept of warranted assertability always has application only at some particular time and place in respect of standards then prevailing. . . . The concept of truth, however, is timeless. To claim that some thesis is true is not only to claim for all possible times and places that it cannot be shown to fail to correspond to reality . . . but also that the mind which expresses its thought in that thesis is in fact adequate to its object. (WJ:363)

According to MacIntyre, practical rationality inhabits a personal and social narrative presupposing that practical truths are discoverable about one's own life and its relations to the Good. Those truths render one's actions intelligible, accountable, evaluable, and thereby befitting a rational moral agent. That agency requires that one be educated into a community of systematic rational enquiry, reenacting those narratives that teach one how to evaluate practical activities and goods. Such communities presuppose shared traditions of understanding and evaluation that recognize practical truths both as independent of and as embodied within those traditions (WJ:196–203).

These enquiries, MacIntyre argues, falsify relativist and perspectivist objections to the rationality of moral traditions, undercutting the contemporary recourse to emotivism. Relativists insist that a tradition's claims are always vindicated from within. In contrast, MacIntyre claims, challenged traditions may recognize rival traditions as possible material for correcting their shortcomings. In such cases, if the borrowed materials permit the borrowing tradition to understand how to resolve its practical problems, the borrowing tradition will be forced to acknowledge the rival's rational superiority. The relativist claim that traditions cannot prove themselves rationally superior, then, also proves false (WJ:364–67).

The rationality of traditions, maintaining that practical truths inhabit their constituent traditions, also defeats the perspectivist challenge. The perspectivist maintains that no claim from within one tradition can falsify claims advanced from other traditions. Yet to adopt one standpoint, MacIntyre maintains, precludes adopting others because it commits one to a view of truth and falsity. The perspectivist, refusing any such commitment, admits no conception of truth adequate to systematic rational enquiry, and is thus excluded from rational debate (WJ:368). Accordingly, MacIntyre concludes, neither perspectivism nor relativism are defensible positions. Rather they represent the vestiges of an emotivist recourse itself bereft of rational justification.

2

MacIntyre on Moral Traditions

Animating MacIntyre's restorative project is his conception of tradition-constituted rationality. That view, however, conceiving rival traditions as incommensurable, undercuts his efforts to combat emotivism and its relativist and perspectivist concomitants. MacIntyre maintains that each moral tradition inhabits a community of discourse and practice, some of whose elements are inherently untranslatable (WJ:373). He claims also that competing traditions must recognize themselves as rivals if one tradition is to rationally vindicate itself vis-à-vis its competitors. If one tradition identifies incoherencies in its rival's positions that the rival's resources cannot explain or correct, for example, then the latter tradition must grant the former's superiority (WJ:388). Yet if standards of truth and rationality are tradition-bound, rival traditions could not appear rational to each other.[1] Moreover, if each tradition maintains coherence by constructing a rational narrative referant to its history alone, admitting alien elements would, in MacIntyre's view, disrupt that enquiry's rational unfolding.

This difficulty is illustrated by MacIntyre's description of contemporary agents as requiring 'conversion' to a functional moral context. According to MacIntyre, modern agents confront a stark choice: adopt a coherent, justified tradition, or remain adrift, inhabiting no viable tradition of practical discourse and holding no justifiable beliefs (WJ:394–95). Agents confronting these options, however, couldn't choose rationally.[2] Their adoption of a previously alien tradition could be justified neither by their previous beliefs, which would then appear irrational, nor by their newly adopted commitments, which could depict that conversion as no better than arational. If, as MacIntyre claims, an intelligible narrative coherently depicts an agent's rational progression toward more adequate beliefs, an initiate's conversion to a superior tradition could appear only as an interruption inexplicable by the narratives that precede and follow it.

That difficulty in sustaining such narrative continuity arises prominently in MacIntyre's own genealogical vindication of his Thomist position. According to MacIntyre, while modern philosophers reject traditional modes of narrative enquiry as truth-constitutive, they nevertheless use the results of those enquiries as "survivals," albeit absent their original authoritative contexts. His genealogy thereby aims to disclose to modern theorists how the emotivist dilemma arises and why they lack the conceptual resources necessary not only to resist, but even to recognize it (FP:57). His account, he claims, thus renders more intelligible than do his rivals' accounts the history of practical enquiry, explaining its deviant episodes and their contemporary consequences (FP:48).

MacIntyre launches his genealogy with his criticism of the Enlightenment: its chief villain—Immanuel Kant. Against Enlightenment thinkers in general and Kant in particular, he charges that they propose ahistorical, universal normative standards hostile to traditional authorities and to the social frameworks practical enquiry ineluctably inhabits. Kant's universalist proceduralism, he suggests, is the worst of the bunch, as it deprives agents' social roles and obligations of moral import and reduces morality to a set of abstract principles (AV:219). Kant's account, he claims, presents a simple and contentless rule, the Categorical Imperative, which renders agents' social situatedness irrelevant to their practical deliberations. For Kant, MacIntyre claims:

> It is of the essence of morality that it lays down principles which are universal, categorical and internally consistent. Hence a rational morality will lay down principles which both can and ought to be held by all men, independent of circumstances and conditions, and which could consistently be obeyed by every rational agent on every occasion. The test for a proposed maxim is then easily framed: can we or can we not consistently will that everyone should always act on it? (AV:43–44)

Given this test, Kant requires practical reasoning to exclude all substantive criteria. It must omit all teleological referents and all referents to practical rationality's historical embeddedness within particular moral communities designating particular obligations and virtues.

MacIntyre's objections, however, misrepresent the teleological function that Kant assigns to practical reason, the nonrational sources that animate it, and its embodiment in a moral community.[3] Kant's moral project unfolds his teleological understanding of human nature, which must be liberated from its egoistic inclinations. In his *Anthropology*, Kant observes that: "From the day that man begins to speak in the first person, he brings his beloved self to light whenever he can, and his egoism advances unrestrained" (AN:10).[4] Conversely he notes: "Egoism can only be contrasted with pluralism, which is a frame of mind in which the self, instead of being enwrapped in itself as if it were the whole world, understands and behaves itself as a mere citizen of the world" (AN:12).

Accordingly, Kant's moral project seeks to make us such citizens. To that end the basic principle underlying his categorical imperative is the premise that one ought to treat other agents always as ends, as subjects of respect, and never merely as means. While the categorical imperative enjoins us to treat other agents with respect, however, it underdetermines what respectful treatment requires. According to his *Grounding for the Metaphysics of Morals*, the categorical imperative entails that we not interfere when others pursue their morally sanctioned ends. Nevertheless Kant contends:

> Now humanity might indeed subsist if nobody contributed anything to the happiness of others, provided he did not intentionally impair their happiness. But this, after all, would harmonize only negatively and not positively with humanity as an end in itself, if everyone does not also strive, as much as he can, to further the ends of others. For the ends of any subject who is an end in himself must as far as possible be my ends also, if that conception of an end in itself is to have its full effect on me. (GR:37/430)[5]

To explain how that conception's "full effect" becomes morally efficacious, Kant posits two classes of duties: the principles of right and the principles of virtue. Under duties of virtue he includes duties to seek one's own perfection and the happiness of others. Serving that latter task discharges the duty of beneficence. Agents must be beneficent, Kant claims, because all agents have happiness as their natural end. Moreover humans are "needful" beings who seek and thus should offer beneficence:

> For every man who finds himself in need wishes that he might be helped by other men. . . . Thus the selfish maxim conflicts with itself when it is made a universal law, i.e. it is contrary to

duty. Consequently, the altrustic maxim of beneficence toward those in need is a universal duty of men; this is so because they are to be regarded as fellow men, i.e. as needy rational beings, united by nature in one dwelling place for mutual aid. (GR:117/453)

According to Kant, since all agents seek happiness and posit ends by which to pursue that happiness, we are obliged to assist them in attaining their ends:

> That beneficence is a duty results from the fact that since our self-love cannot be separated from our need to be loved by others (to obtain help from them in case of need), we therefore make ourselves an end for others; and this maxim can never be obligatory except by qualifying as a universal law and, consequently, through a will to make others our ends. Hence the happiness of others is an end which is at the same time a duty. (MPV:52/393)[6]

Yet such claims, referring essentially to agents not only rational but also needful, irremediably conflate the empirical desires most humans share, for example, happiness, with the a priori conception of a rational being. That conflation has had two major implications for subsequent developments of Kant's project. First, given Kant's account of these "imperfect" duties, beneficence and other virtues cannot be optional expressions of autonomy. Rather we must cultivate them as conditions of autonomy, as conditions that free agents from their egoism.[7] Deficiencies in these virtues are thus no less objectionable than deficiencies in our "perfect" duties. Accordingly, the categorical imperative must admit empirical ends indicating imperfect duties and the virtues they enjoin.[8]

For that reason, the question of how practical reason becomes morally efficacious can only be answered definitively at the social level. Conjointly reason and natural inclination draw agents into social interactions bounded by duties limning a particular community, Kant's Kingdom of Ends. Indeed, the interplay between perfect and imperfect duties suggests that for Kant imperfect duties and the virtues they commend function as dispositional categories of moral judgment, as deliberative mechanisms agents must cultivate to realize the moral community he envisioned.[9] On this account, virtues and the inclinations they rationalize develop practical reason as a social practice which conditions how, indeed whether, agents realize the Kingdom of Ends.

Realizing that community requires agents not to disavow but to improve upon their nature, to make it more perfect than nature created it. That process, Kant stresses, requires agents to exercise autonomy not merely by performing their perfect duties but by cultivating those virtues that direct their inclinations toward appropriate ends. Such a community requires a particular practice of practical reasoning, a social practice of deliberative judgment including both perfect and imperfect duties, the latter fostering those virtues which operate as 'categories' of moral judgment. These virtues and the imperfect duties to which they accord, then, both procedurally and substantively limn the deliberative field, specifying the communal ends to which individual ends and principles are subordinate.

On these points the Kantian tradition evinces significantly more continuity with the Aristotelean tradition than MacIntyre acknowledges. Like Aristotle, Kant offers a teleological accounting of how human nature can be perfected. Also like Aristotle's, Kant's account rationalizes the contemporary moral standards he met; Kant was no more a moral revolutionary than was Aristotle. Moreover, like Aristotle, Kant offers us a decision procedure for evaluating means and ends that is strictly limited by communal requirements and by the duties and virtues requisite to sustaining such a community. Indeed, Kant is no less determinative than is Aristotle in detailing the virtues that such a moral community must embody.

More importantly, despite differences among the specific virtues they commend, their conceptions of practical rationality are closely analogous in structure and function. Much as Aristotle specifies a 'rule'—the golden mean—and a set of virtues conducing to a community resolving individual and social pursuits, Kant's categorical imperative also specifies a rule and a set of virtues tending to a community reconciling such pursuits. Their accounts differ on the extent to which such pursuits must be thus reconciled, of course. But that difference is one of degree rather than, as MacIntyre suggests, of kind. The difference is a matter of emphasis, Aristotle upon community, Kant upon autonomy. Yet both identify appropriate human ends delimiting the moral communities they envision. To this extent, for Kant as for Aristotle the right and the good are inseparable. For Aristotle, these converge in the polis, for Kant in the Kingdom of Ends.

Virtue Traditions: Ancient and Modern

While MacIntyre's genealogy overemphasizes the discontinuities between the Kantian and Aristotelean traditions, it underestimates the Thomist tradition's continuity with the history of practical enquiry. That distortion is most evident in MacIntyre's extended contrast between the Scottish Enlightenment and what he terms the Thomist synthesis. According to MacIntyre, the traditions Aquinas integrated, despite their discontinuities, exhibited broad commonalities among their conceptions of teleology, of practical reasoning, and of the good life. Specifically, he claims, both the Aristotelean and the Augustinean traditions afforded teleologies orienting practical reason toward a determinate conception of the Good. Aquinas' enquiries thus built upon substantial practical agreements.

In that way Aquinas' task differed sharply from that of the Scottish Enlightenment's theorists, who confronted extensive practical disagreement spawned by political and economic change. These changes loosened previous linkages between individual and social interests such that the overriding question for these theorists became how competing goods could coexist, given broad agreement that no univocal hierarchy of goods obtained. During the Scottish Enlightenment, MacIntyre claims, this debate sparked disputes between Christians who maintained that theological principles properly subordinated individual to communal interests, and secularists who premised their ideal social order upon individuals' self-interested pursuits (WJ:212–13).

The competing positions relevant here are exemplified by three theorists: Viscount Stair, Francis Hutchenson, and David Hume. Stair, MacIntyre claims, represents the classical position of the Scottish Enlightenment, maintaining that theological principles are independent of and rightly subordinate individual interests, particularly propertied interests, to the common good (WJ:252–59). Later thinkers, however, particularly Hutchenson, confronted a social and economic climate in which theology came under increasing pressure to accommodate commercial interests. Hutchenson's "unstable compromise," as MacIntyre terms it, sought to resolve these interests by uniting theology and natural philosophy.

Hutchenson fused these interests by positing a 'moral sense' that regulated natural egoistic and altruistic motives. That sense grounded rational theological principles in common feelings guiding the exercise of natural law and supplying substantive grounds for just social agreements. Such a synthesis was inherently unstable, as it founded traditional ideas of natural law and morality upon a novel conception of human nature. As successors such as Hume showed, Hutchenson's theological principles were deeply incompatible with his moral epistemology, such that only one or the other might survive (WJ:270–80). Inevitably, MacIntyre maintains, Hutchenson's synthesis gave way to Hume's skepticism.

In contrast, MacIntyre argues, Aquinas' synthesis faltered not because it embodied incongruous elements but because his successors abandoned his view of practical enquiry as inhabiting a systematic, narrative tradition of enquiry (TRV:150–51). That loss resulted from institutional and curricular changes that deprived practical enquiry of its systematic unity, fostering independent disciplines militating against Aquinas' synthetic methodology. Absent that unity, practical enquiry became an autonomous discipline, supplying its own rational standards independent of essential theological reference. These social changes, MacIntyre claims, compounded by political disputes that intensified as the theological basis of practical enquiry unraveled, led Aquinas' synthesis to falter by the fourteenth century (TRV:165–69).

MacIntyre's genealogy, however, never shows how the decline of Aquinas' synthesis differs in principle from that of Hutchenson's. Both syntheses confront secular challenges to their theological accounts of practical enquiry, and of justice, that assailed their integrity as traditions. Moreover, while MacIntyre's genealogy stresses the disparate elements Hutchenson integrates, it never acknowledges the deep divisions between Aquinas and Aristotle, divisions at least as prominent as those he alleges between Aristotle and Kant. Both Aristotle and Kant, after all, develop secular accounts of practical rationality and of justice that commend similar virtues and similar functions for practical rationality. In contrast, Aquinas affirms novel virtues, humility for example, inimical to the Aristotelean tradition, and proposes a universalist conception of justice no more continuous with Aristotle's than is Kant's.

The discontinuities among all of these traditions, however, should not obscure their continuities. Such continuities are denied by MacIntyre's genealogy, which suggests, for example, that recent efforts to develop a Thomist conception of 'natural rights' signify 'alien' modern additions to Aquinas' synthesis rather than its natural outgrowths (TRV:76). Yet that claim overlooks the conflict between secular and theological conceptions of justice that Aquinas like Hutchenson faced, a confrontation arising from the theological requirement that justice extend throughout the moral community he envisioned (WJ:199–202). It also overlooks how deeply rooted the central concepts of the natural rights tradition are in theological and teleological concepts Aquinas helped to develop. Indeed, Aquinas' system must harbor such resources to secure one of its goals, secular justice, and to exemplify the dialectical development MacIntyre claims marks well-ordered traditions.

Such an account would see natural rights not as unintelligible artifacts of an unintelligible project, but as developments of a continuous tradition of practical enquiry including Aquinas as a central participant. MacIntyre would reject that conclusion on the ground that modern and premodern modes of practical enquiry are discontinuous, a rupture signaled by modern theorists' hostility to teleology, to tradition, and to substantive truth claims. MacIntyre's position, however, signals an analogous hostility, for in denying substantive continuities among the modern and premodern traditions, he distorts the history of practical enquiry, distorts how that history harbors traditions, and distorts the conception of truth this shared history indicates.

Neither Aristotle, nor Aquinas, nor Kant aimed to establish standards of truth and rationality wholly devoid of traditional referents. They sought to afford universal normative standards that they took to vindicate "common knowledge." Given this effort, moral traditions become neither wholly authoritative nor wholly dispensable, but sources of constructive material. More importantly, this material is never isolated, as MacIntyre suggests, from the traditions that contribute to it. Rather, as his own genealogy implies, traditions seed each other, their cross-currents challenge each other, and the social, historical, and cultural contingencies they mutually endure condition their successes and failures.

As these traditions retain inheritances neither wholly authoritative nor wholly dispensable, and as they harbor broadly communicable concepts, for example, justice however conceived, the normative standards they propose will embody both local and nonlocal references. Those standards will arise amid particular traditions but employ conceptual resources inherited from and distributed among other traditions and thus referant to practical realities transcending particular traditions. That distribution of partially shared resources undermines MacIntyre's conception of insular traditions, which alone are alleged to harbor practical truths. Yet such a distribution of conceptual resources is implied by MacIntyre's own position, which wavers between a view of rational enquiry tradition-bound to the point of solipsism, and realist to the point that it's unclear how any tradition could enclose truth as he conceives it in toto.

Perspectivism and Practical Enquiry

That wavering between the tradition-bound and the tradition-independent texture of practical claims replicates in MacIntyre's position a tension between tradition and truth that is endemic to the Enlightenment. It arises in MacIntyre's account because his assertion of the primacy of tradition-bound rationality rejects any view of transhistorical truth, a vision to which Aquinas and Aristotle themselves give expression.[10] MacIntyre's genealogy, for example, isolates the premodern traditions he avers from the modern traditions they spawned. Denying the continuities among such traditions, however, undermines his claim that substantive continuity obtains between the Aristotelean and the Thomist traditions, given the extent to which he claims that truth and rationality are tradition-bound and tradition-constituted.

More importantly, his account alienates the traditions he avers from the history of practical enquiry, isolating them from their competitors and reenforcing the relativism and perspectivism he rejects. If truth and rationality are wholly bound to traditions, those traditions' adherents would have no rational basis for evaluating their own truth claims. Rather, those claims would prove strictly self-validating. In contrast, if practical truths transcend individual traditions, it's unclear how any single tradition could afford the univocal locus of truth.[11] MacIntyre claims that truth is both independent of and constituted by the Thomist tradition. The independence of that truth, he maintains, falsifies the relativist claim that such traditions are self-vindicating, whereas that truth's localization defeats the perspectivist claim that no particular tradition can embody universal truths.

MacIntyre's account of truth, however, affirming that truth claims can be falsified transtraditionally, seemingly presupposes a perspectivism of its own, albeit a form quite different from the Nietzschean version he rejects (TRV:36–40). Absent a perspectivist position, that is, either the claim that truth is tradition-constituted, or the claim that truth is tradition-independent, must be surrendered. Were the former claim maintained, traditions could not rationally confront each other. Were the latter claim maintained, practical claims could not be transtraditionally falsifiable, hence could not secure the vindication MacIntyre maintains they must.[12] Indeed, MacIntyre's account of tradition-constituted rationality can be marshalled against relativism and perspectivism only if such traditions accord partial truths, to which other traditions bear joint witness as a condition of their rational engagement.[13]

MacIntyre's account of narrative truth, of course, requires that practical claims be reconciled such that one tradition harbors substantive truth. That locus underlies his claim that the narratives agents inhabit must be true for their actions to be intelligible and evaluable. While he describes agents' narratives as "aspiring to truth," however, were those aspirations unfulfilled, such narratives would not admit of strict truth or falsity. Rather, the truth or falsity they embodied would be contextualized, referring to a reality not independent of the evaluators but constructed through their narratives.

That conclusion is fully consonant with MacIntyre's claim that agency is possible only within tradition-referant narratives. Yet these narratives do not refer unilaterally to any one set of facts independent of the narrative. Rather, agents' narratives select, thematize, and array these facts. Such thematizations underlie the fluidity of possible narratives, whose constituent facts become more or less prominent as they jostle for position within our historical typographies. As these facts assume different roles within such narratives, however, we have no independent basis for selecting one sequence as uniquely factual, uniquely real.[14] Rather, the real sequence is that sequence efficacious in the present, whatever its objective position within the narrative.

At the same time, the facts of our lives remain so however we choose to thematize them. The irreducibility of those facts to any particular narrative would on MacIntyre's view render those facts unintelligible. Yet even granting that those facts acquire intelligibility only within some narrative, that texture does not guarantee any particular narrative's univocal truth. That difficulty, however, does not forbid such narratives being true not in a realist but in a coherentist sense. Truth or falsity, that is, might then accrue to socially constructed facts. MacIntyre's account suggests such a constructivist orientation given its emphasis upon traditions' power to underwrite agents' narratives. Objective evaluation would then arise not from the facts of human nature, but from the facts of human social orders. This approach, however, lacks both the internal coherence and the objective referents defining Aristotle's approach, referents that for Aristotle univocally selected out specific narratives as commendable.[15] The constructivist thrust of MacIntyre's project, then, no more supplies objective referents for moral evaluations than does its realist orientation.

MacIntyre's account of practical truth lingers between constructivism and realism, failing on its own terms to distinguish true from false moral premises. His account lingers between these positions for two reasons. First, in rejecting Aristotle's metaphysical biology and its transhistorical thrust in favor of a tradition-centered account of practical rationality, MacIntyre circumscribes truth wholly within particular traditions. Second, his conception of practical enquiry requires faith in tradition-constituted truths, including revealed truths, reference to which sustains both its individual and collective narratives. According to MacIntyre, this tradition's immanent epistemology is realist, approximating to truth dialectically within the confines of revealed tradition.

Yet that dialectical unfolding accords with a sense of truth neither realist nor constructivist, neither tradition-independent nor tradition-constituted. Within the Thomist tradition, the human mind conforms to a truth anterior to itself. At the same time, that truth is unavailable to those who do not inhabit the requisite tradition. Its very localization within a tradition apart from which it cannot become available, however, implies that truth's constructivist dimension. On such an account, the truth that this tradition makes available will not, as MacIntyre insists, be discovered, but will be both given and created.

To the extent that the truths of that tradition are both discovered and constructed, ultimate authority attends neither source. To grant the realist element such authority would imply its tradition-independence, its accessability even to enquirers inhabiting other traditions, an accessability MacIntyre's conception of tradition-constituted rationality denies. Yet to assign the constructivist element such authority would enclose the tradition's adherents within that tradition, unable to encounter rivals, as the relativist charges. According to MacIntyre, the relativist grants no rational recourse across traditions, whereas the perspectivist grants no truth claims within any one tradition. MacIntyre's account, lingering between realism and constructivism, flirts with both of these positions. Indeed, his account must render truth neither wholly immanent to the tradition he espouses, nor wholly external to that tradition, if it is to defeat the twin challenges of perspectivism and relativism.

In confining truth to a single tradition, however, MacIntyre falsely segregates premodern and modern traditions, misassessing the broader teleology they mutually unfold. His genealogy founders on his denial of transtraditional truths and on his insistence that practical truth resides not within traditions but within a particular tradition. He claims, for example, that ethnocentrism is the norm for traditions, which can only be compared and contrasted as wholes (WJ:28,77). He even recognizes the challenge theological traditions face when asserting that faith is a necessary precursor to rational enquiry (WJ:146). Yet he insists, against the relativist, that rival traditions' claims must become data for other traditions' dialectical investigations, as a condition of their potential engagements.

At the same time, he argues against the perspectivist that truth is integral to traditions, such that adopting one standpoint commits one to a view of truth and falsity to which a multiplicity of truth standards is antagonstic (WJ:367–68). Because perspectivists are uncommitted to a univocal conception of truth, he insists, they employ no rational standards adequate to systematic enquiry (WJ:368). Accordingly, he argues against the relativist that truth is objective and timeless, and against the perspectivist that truth is tradition-bound. These claims, however, can be rendered intelligible neither from within one tradition alone nor apart from all traditions, but only from within a broader multi-faceted tradition whose shared resources might reveal the truths he seeks.

3

Traditions of Enquiry

A Whiteheadian Alternative

MacIntyre's effort to defeat perspectivism founders in part because he identifies that position with Nietzsche's antimetaphysical perspectivism. More importantly, like both his Enlightenment-inspired and genealogical rivals, he rejects explicitly metaphysical modes of enquiry. Yet that refusal undermines his accounts of truth, tradition, and practical rationality, which neither appropriately diagnose the contemporary emotivist recourse nor propose persuasive solutions to the challenges that recourse presents. Such modes of enquiry, however, as developed for example by Alfred North Whitehead, offer a contemporary alternative MacIntyre ignores. That alternative is consonant with MacIntyre's project on several major points, yet affords a more coherent accounting of the interrelations among tradition, truth, and practical rationality than MacIntyre's accounts offer.

Like MacIntyre, Whitehead espouses a teleological mode of enquiry which requires us to fully characterize the "complete facts" we encounter. Such characterizations are not offered by modern investigative techniques that reject final causes. Those methods can neither explain nor deny the natural purposiveness biological phenomena evince by reference to physical law alone. In trying to do so, we would commit what Whitehead terms "the fallacy of misplaced concreteness," that is, we would mistake a partial analysis for a complete analysis.[1] In contrast, to explain the interweaving of efficient and final causes the natural world exhibits we must avoid segregating facts and values: "We must conceive each actuality as attaining an end for itself. . . . This is the doctrine that each actuality is an occasion of experience, the outcome of its own purposes" (FR:24–25).[2]

According to Whitehead, occasions of experience actualize values as they become facts. They are microscopic organisms, "drops of experience, complex and interdependent" each uniting its actual world from its own perspective (PR:231–32).[3] Their individual unities or concrescences arise from their creative syntheses of the formative elements (data) they prehend: other actual occasions, universals (eternal objects), and God. During their formation actual occasions apprehend these formative elements via "vector feelings," appropriations by which they integrate the data they encounter into their distinctive unities of subjective form. Each actuality physically inherits from its past data upon which it must render a novel decision (PR:43–47). Those data include not only physical inheritances but also the eternal objects or forms of definiteness actualities reproduce via their 'decisions': "Each actuality is essentially bipolar, physical and mental, and the physical inheritance is essentially accompanied by a conceptual reaction partly conformed to it, and partly introductory of a relevant novel contrast, but always introducing emphasis, valuation, and purpose" (PR:108). Through their decisions or self-constitutions, each actual occasion transits from selectively appropriating its physical inheritances and its ideal possibilities to enjoying the results of that appropriative activity. These satisfactions becoming the "final facts," "the final real things" (RM:101–2).

Yet those satisfactions could not be effected absent their third formative element: God. To effect their satisfactions, occasions appropriate eternal objects, which both lend determinancy to and lay down patterns of definiteness whereby occasions prehend each other.[4] Eternal objects, however, would remain inert potentials unless continuously "ingressed" in actualities. Moreover, Whitehead argues, eternal objects must have their relevance to the occasions "graded" before they can become effective in individual decisions, a task accomplished through God's conceptual valuation of them. Every creative act thus presupposes God's initial creative act, His conceptual realization and gradation of all potential values, as a condition of its own realization. At the same time, each actual entity derives from God its basic conceptual aim, yet with indeterminations awaiting its own decisions. Thereby, God supplies the occasion's initial subjective aim as a "lure" to induce that occasion to realize His own aims: novelty, harmony, and intensity of value: "This is the conception of God, according to which He is considered as the outcome of creativity, as the foundation of order, and as the goad towards novelty."[5, 6]

For Whitehead, then, as for MacIntyre, God affords that initial patterning of value absent which the universe would lack valuative potential. Moreover, God's influence extends to each concrescent's agent capacity as well as to the objective conditions of that agency. Each occasion depends for its self-completion not only upon God's initial gradation of eternal objects, but also upon the "subjective aim" or initial purpose that it inherits from its predecessors via God's conceptaul valuations. Every actual entity thereby exhibits a triadic character: (1) an objective inheritance, (2) a subjective decision transmitting that inheritance into a novel fact, and (3) a superjective legacy, the "objective immortality" by which novel facts condition creative acts beyond their originating decisions. According to Whitehead:

> In its self-creation the actual entity is guided by its ideal of itself as individual satisfaction and as transcendent creator. The enjoyment of this ideal is the "subjective aim," by reason of which the actual entity is a determinant process. (PR:85)

That subjective aim is inherited from God and conditioned by the other formative elements constituting each entity's actual world. Nevertheless, essential novelty attaches to how individuals appropriate these data: "These subjective ways of feeling are not merely receptive of the data as alien facts; they clothe the dry bones with the flesh of a real being, emotional, purposive, appreciative" (PR:85). Each actuality, then, "is finally responsible for the decision by which any lure for feeling is admitted to efficiency. The freedom inherent in the universe is constituted by this element of self-causation" (PR:88). This interplay between God and actualities, Whitehead maintains, illustrates the latters' essential reference to the former:

> The religious insight is the grasp of this truth: That the universe exhibits a creativity with infinite freedom, and a realm of forms with infinite possibilities; but that this creativity and these forms are together impotent to achieve actuality apart from the completed ideal harmony, which is God. (RM:119–20)[7]

Speculative and Practical Reason

In developing his teleology Whitehead shares with MacIntyre several theoretical orientations: his grounding of rational enquiry within a theological framework, his grounding of agency within a teleology according to God's valuations, and his grounding of rationality as immanent within that framework and as approximating toward its own ends. Whitehead's conception of the universe's creativity, however, conditions his accounts of agency, rationality, and truth such that he describes the progress of enquiry into that teleology quite differently than does MacIntyre.

That divergence shows itself initially in how Whitehead relates speculative and practical reason.[8] Whitehead maintains that rational enquiry uncovers a theological apprehension of the universe's character, whose most fundamental religious concepts are the nature of God and the aim of life (RM:86, 139). Moreover, like MacIntyre, he acknowledges the centrality of a dogmatic context—of a tradition—within which to conduct such investigations. Nevertheless he claims: "The foundations of dogma must be laid in a rational metaphysics which . . . endeavors to express the most general concepts adequate for the all-inclusive universe" (RM:83). To that end such enquiries must test religious truth as they test other kinds of truths: "so as to absorb into one system all sources of experience" (RM:124, 149).

This endeavor, he claims, reveals that:

> The importance of rational religion in the history of modern culture is that it stands or falls with its fundamental position, that we know more than can be formulated in one finite systematized scheme of abstraction, however important that scheme may be in the elucidation of some aspect of the order of things. (RM:143)

According to Whitehead while traditions harbor truths, they risk perpetrating falsehoods when they refuse to evolve as do the enquiries sustaining them. Traditions, selective of the evidences they admit, are inevitably limited in their potential to yield true judgments, and perpetrate falsehoods if they fail to acknowledge their conceptual limits. Finite formulations cannot offer complete truths but can only grow in proportion of truth: "Progress in truth . . . is mainly a progress in the framing of concepts, in discarding artificial abstractions or partial metaphors, and in evolving notions which strike more deeply into the root of reality" (RM:131, 149). An enquiry undertaken within a dogmatic tradition may assist this process if it doesn't exceed its conceptual limits: "But if the same dogma be used intolerantly so as to check the employment of other modes of analyzing the subject matter, then, for all its truth, it will be doing the work of falsehood" (RM:131).

Traditions dogmatically defended inevitably issue in falsehood; were that not so, rational religion itself would not have progressed. Whitehead traces the development of that religion from ritual to belief to rationalization, claiming that each stage succeeded the other when its prior forms could no longer contain the conceptual possibilities newly available. Such, for example, was the outcome of the Thomist synthesis to which MacIntyre claims allegiance. That stage in Christianity's development, Whitehead maintains, hovers between tribalism and universality, rationalizing the Hebrew religion's insight into the nature of things, specifically that nature's moral order, while according that nature to a 'barbaric' god (RM:54–55). Such a religion served well as a progressive social ideal, eliciting cognate ideals of moral agency and responsibility. Yet this tradition surrendered its progressive potential as it came to rely upon intellectually isolated, backward-looking modes of enquiry. Then, he claims:

> They [medieval theorists] were salvaging the old virtues which had made the race the great race that it had been, and were not straining forward towards the new virtues to make the common life the City of God that it should be. They were religions of the average, and the average is at war with the ideal. (RM:39)

Such enquiries were at war with the ideal because they misconstrued the appropriate relation between speculative and practical enquiry. For Whitehead reason unfurls both as a function of an animal body and as abstractive from any such function: "There is Reason, asserting itself as above the world, and there is Reason as one of many factors within the world" (FR:6–7). To its practical function he assigns the task of developing those methods and traditions embodying specific enquiries. Yet such methods countenance the likelihood of dogmatic misuse: "Reason which is methodic is content to limit itself within the bounds of a successful method. It works in the secure daylight of traditional practical activity" (FR:51). In contrast:

> The speculative Reason is in its essence untrammelled by method. Its function is to pierce into the general reasons beyond limited reasons, to understand all methods as coordinated in a nature of things only to be grasped by transcending all method. (FR:51)

Here, Whitehead refers to scientific methods as well as to traditions of practical enquiry. All such methods exhibit similar life histories, progressing from their original conceptions, to their wide and satisfactory coordinations of thought and action, to their conceptual exhaustions (FR:14). The initial stage of such methods signifies their novel achievement, whereas their last stage signifies a conceptual lassitude compromising their potential to evoke novel valuations. Practical enquiries, Whitehead maintains, embody three aims: the urge to live, the urge to live well, and the urge to live better. Inevitably, however, every such enquiry confronts a choice between advance and regression as a consequence of its own success:

> In its prime it satisfies the immediate conditions for the good life. But the good life is unstable: the law of fatigue is inexorable. When any methodology of life has exhausted the novelties within its scope and played upon them up to the incoming of fatigue, one final decision determines the fate of a species. It can stabilize itself, and relapse so as to live; or it can shake itself free, and enter upon the adventure of living better. (FR:14)

At the height of their success these methods offer repetitive structures and ordered frameworks within which agents enjoy complex and varied patterns of experience. Yet those enjoyments are temporary achievements whose potential is threatened by the method's success: "The meridian triumph of a method is when it facilitates opportunity without any transcending of itself" (FR:18).

At its worst, such stabilization represents dogmatic relapse to prior achievements. Such was the fate of the Scholastics, whose insistence upon the dogmatic finality of their first principles set speculative and practical reason irremediably at odds. Scholasticism underestimated the "fecundity" of nature and thought: "It formed a closed system of thinking about other people's thoughts" (FR:35). The Scholastics framed their metaphysical systems from a narrow range of ideas and of meditation upon those ideas sans contact with novel experience (FR:34–37, 57–58). That stagnation undermined Scholasticism when it confronted new challenges. Then, its dialectical acuteness and rigid systematization deprived it of the conceptual resources it required to reconstruct itself, as evidenced by the Scholastics' refusal to speculate freely on the limits of their methods:

But there is a strict limit to the utility of any finite scheme. If the scheme be pressed beyond its proper scope, definite error results. The art of speculative Reason consists quite as much in the transcendence of schemes as in their utilization. (FR:60)

Such transcendence is necessary because "Every construction of human intelligence is more special, more limited than was its original aim" (FR:70). At the same time, speculative reason "is driven forward by the ultimate faith that each particular fact is understandable as illustrating the general principles of its own nature and of its status among other particular facts. It fulfills its function when understanding has been gained" (FR:29). In that pursuit, rejecting any source of evidence contravenes an enquiry's rational progress. Moreover that progress requires a futural orientation inimical to dogmatic recourse. Reason elucidates both itself and its methods in pursuit of its aim: "Its business is to make thought creative of the future" (FR:65). Practical methods are the mechanism whereby reason accomplishes that task, yet those methods have shelf lives, limitations suggesting that the most any tradition can accomplish is to "[convert] the decay of one order into the birth of its successor" (FR:72). To that end:

The true use of history is that we extract from it general principles as to the discipline of practice and the discipline of speculation. The object of this discipline is not stability but progress. . . . What looks like stability is a relatively slow process of atrophied decay. The stable universe is slipping away from under us. Our aim is upward. (FR:66)

Practical methodologies must aim upwards because "The function of Reason is to promote the art of life" (FR:2). For Whitehead practical reason embodies a tripartite aim: to live, to live well and to live better (FR:5). Underwriting practical enquiries' progress is God's ordered provision of conceptual possibilities evoking novel enjoyments. As such order is teleologically rooted in experience, the order God establishes is an objective referent for such enquiries. At the same time, for Whitehead "All order is . . . aesthetic order, and the moral order is merely certain aspects of aesthetic order" (RM:105). Whitehead's subordination of other modes of order to aesthetic order thus underlies his account of how practical methodologies are developed, sustained, and justified.

According to Whitehead, God's primordial nature envisages all elements of the traditional normative triumverate—truth, beauty, and goodness. That envisagement induces those patterned activities by which individuals realize the ends God proposes. Individuals are thus enjoined to reproduce the valuations they inherit, inheritances that the preestablished harmony between God and the world permits. That preestablished harmony, however, is reconstructed by individuals' decisions upon their inheritances. Every actual entity inherits from God an initial "subjective aim," a conceptual appetition in the form of a "proposition" that depends upon the individual's decision for its realization: "The preestablished harmony is the self-consistency of this proposition, that is to say, its capacity for realization" (PR:224) While the individual decision remains suspended, the proposition realizes neither truth, nor beauty, nor goodness. Thus unrealized, propositions function as "primitive theories," and "the primary function of theories is as a lure for feeling, thereby providing immediacy of enjoyment and purpose" (PR:184).

Those lures must induce subjects, the actualities entertaining those propositions, to realize those propositions, because only individuals' decisions convert possibilities into facts. Actual entities thus serve as co-creators of the world they and God constitute. The normative patterns that world realizes, as well as the conditions of those patterns' realizations, are their mutual products. God affords the initial envisagement, the patterned potentials, and the propositions enticing those potentials' enactments. Yet those potentials pass over to the actualities that decide their efficacy. Those decisions lay down objective patterns for later decisions, patterns secured in God's Consequent nature and reproduced by individuals' successors to the extent that those patterns offer enduring possibilities for novel satisfactions. The normative patterns governing those satisfactions are multiply located, both in God and in the world, and evolve in tandem. Moreover, as this interaction is co-created, God's valuations are not uniquely determinative of an overriding normative order: His function in inducing valuation is not commanding but persuasive.

On Whitehead's account, then, normative standards, whether of truth, beauty, or goodness, while objectively haunting this shared world, endure only as they remain persuasive, and must evolve to retain their efficacy. Thereby they exemplify Whitehead's claim that standards of truth and of goodness are subordinate to the aesthetic ends God proposes: novelty, intensity, and harmony of valuation. The objectivity of all such standards, Whitehead maintains, signifies their subservience to aesthetic ends. Truth conditions, for. example, are localized jointly in God and in the world, attaching individuals to other individuals and to God through their mutual reproductions of a shared world. At the same time, those conditions limn how the propositions effective in that world will become effective for the future, transforming those conditions in the process of realizing them.

Practical Reasoning and Aesthetic Order

The truth conditions God envisages thus refer to additional actualities, rendering his specifications inherently incomplete: "All entities, including even other actual entities, enter into the self-realization of an actuality in the capacity of determinants of the definiteness of that actuality. By reason of this objective functioning of entities there is truth and falsehood" (PR:223). God's specifications alone cannot render individuals' decisions wholly indicative of truth or falsehood, of their conformity or nonconformity to the mutually constructed world order. Rather: "Truth and falsehood always require some element of sheer givenness. . . . The subjects of a proposition supply the element of givenness requisite for truth and falsehood" (PR:258–59).

One element in that givenness is actualities' proposal of novel truth conditions. The truth conditions God proposes entail creatures' creativity. His initial propositions induce objective conformity—truthful, beautiful, and good—to His ideals. Yet each normative aspect of that conformity signifies a novel pattern of emotional integration attaching not to a proposition's realized but to its potential truth: "Every proposition presupposes those actual entities which are its logical subjects. . . . The proposition itself awaits its logical subjects. Thus propositions grow with the creative advance of the world" (PR:188). As those propositions yield truths, they realize novel propositions whose content is irreducible to their original proposals: "Evidently new propositions come into being with the creative advance of the world. For every proposition involves its logical subjects; and it cannot be the proposition which it is, unless those logical subjects are the actual entities which they are" (PR:259).

As those propositions and the norms they realize accord to God's aesthetic ends, the truth conditions thus specified must exemplify that order. All elements of the traditional triumvirate of truth, beauty, and goodness hold out valuative potential. Yet truth and goodness, Whitehead maintains, owe that potential to aesthetic valuation and so serve its ends above their own. For Whitehead, truth relations take many forms. Besides traditional correspondence and coherence modes, truth may also take the form of symbolic reference, signifying not causal linkages between predicates' subjective entertainments and their objective embodiments, but a community of subjective form approximating to a social reality, a historical truth for instance (AI:319–20).[9] Moreover, truth can also be represented by proper bodily function, that function evincing the conformity of part to whole denoting aesthetic order (AI:316–17). In each instantiation, truth relations qualify aspects of the subject's apprehension of the object. At the same time, these truth modes all presuppose relations that extend beyond the bare truth relation, instead embodying the mutual adaptation of parts to wholes that marks aesthetic order with its aims at the harmony and intensity of novel satisfactions.

To that end, truth relations narrowly construed, as in formally logical procedures permitting merely two options for decision upon a proposition—true or false—are of limited use. Worse still, such truth relations preclude propositions, false from some limited perspective, which might prove productive of value. In contrast, he claims: "It is more important that a proposition be interesting than that it be true," interesting in that it can incite novel conceptual responses in its primary function—as a lure for feeling (AI:313). While interesting propositions are of such import, Whitehead grants, those eliciting substantive valuative potential may well more likely prove true than false. Still he claims: "It is an erroneous moral platitude, that it is necessarily good to know the truth. The minor truth may beget the major evil" (AI:311). Minor truths beget evil when they overstep their bounds, claiming for their perfections an authoritative status unavailable to them, and undermining the valuative potential of alternative propositions. Finite truths, Whitehead claims, whatever their merits in their restricted domains, must give way to the aesthetic order's creative advance: "Apart from Beauty, Truth is neither good, nor bad. . . . Beauty is left as the one aim which by its nature is self-justifying" (AI:342).

The claim that restricted truths must give way to the aesthetic order underlies Whitehead's conception of practical reason's function. Its role is not primarily to recreate past achievements, inherited patterns of valuations, or practical methodologies, but to propose novel ideals for the realization of new perfections. Univocal commitment to practical truths confined to narrow traditions and eliciting few novel enjoyments undermines practical reason's task in two ways. First, such commitments risk abandoning the pursuit of future valuative potential to current or past achievements. Second, those commitments wed practical enquiry to a conception of truth inimical to its own ends.

Practical enquiry faces those risks when its perfections no longer hold out the potential they once did for novel valuation. Of the Greeks' attainments, for example, Whitehead notes that despite the inheritance they left, their original achievements stagnated at the hands of their successors, who refused to admit novel practical possibilities. The Greeks perfected one form of civilization: "But even perfection will not bear the tedium of indefinite repetition. To sustain a civilization with the intensity of its first ardor requires more than learning. Adventure is essential, namely, the search for new perfections" (AI:322). Moreover, the Greeks would hardly adduce the backward-looking claims often advanced on their behalf: "Compared to their neighbors, they were singularly unhistorical. They were speculative, adventurous, eager for novelty. The most un-Greek thing that we can do is to copy the Greeks. For emphatically they were not copyists" (AI:353).

Rather, if we are to properly tend that inheritance: "It really is not sufficient to direct attention to the best that has been said and done in the ancient world. The result is static, repressive, and promotes a decadent habit of mind" (AI:352–53). It promotes a decadent habit of mind because:

> The foundation of all understanding of sociological theory—that is to say, of all understanding of human life—is that no static maintenance of perfection is possible. This axiom is rooted in the nature of things. Advance or decadence are the only choices offered to mankind. The pure conservative is fighting against the essence of the universe. (AI:353–54)

Such conservativism threatens the foundation of the moral enterprise, a project oriented essentially toward its future valuative possibilities:

> The effect of the present on the future is the business of morals. . . . Thus stagnation is the deadly foe of morality. Yet in human society the champions of morality are on the whole the fierce opponents of new ideals. Mankind has been afflicted with low toned moralists, objecting to expulsion from some Garden of Eden. (AI:346)

The problem with rejecting such new ideals is not that they always improve upon older ideals, nor even that they always prove more conformal to the aesthetic order's creative advance, but that they offer possibilities that can only be tested via their realizations. Traditions unfold these ideals through three stages: (1) romance, wherein they elicit the excitement of novel valuative possibilities, (2) precision, wherein they discipline knowledge and action for sustained value realization, and (3) generalization, wherein they distill from that precision perfections of potentially enduring relevance to their successors. Here, traditions both attain their full valuative potential, and encounter their conceptual limits: "This finiteness is not the result of evil, or of imperfection. It results from the fact that there are possibilities of harmony which either produce evil in joint realization, or are incapable of such conjunction" (AI:356).

This finitude marks the valuative selections by which civilizations incarnate their unique perfections: "Thus in every civilization at its culmination we should find a large measure of realization of a certain type of perfection" (AI:357). Yet traditions sustain that apex only if they admit novel valuative possibilities: "The culmination can maintain itself at its height so long as fresh experimentation within the type is possible" (AI:357). If that condition is subordinated to the maintenance of past or current ideals, imagination withers: "Staleness then sets in. Repetition produces a gradual lowering of vivid appreciation. Convention dominates. A learned orthodoxy suppresses adventure" (AI:358). And as imagination atrophies, civilizations founder: "A race preserves its vigour so long as it harbors a real contrast between what has been and what may be; and so long as it is nerved by the vigour to adventure beyond the safeties of the past. Without adventure civilization is in full decay" (PR:360).

Recourse to learned orthodoxy signifies not the apex of such a civilization but the waning of its capacity to elicit novel valuations: "The prolongation of outworn forms of life means a slow decadence in which there is repetition without any fruit in the reaping of value" (AI:359). Those forms of life render thought recapitulative of the past rather than creative of the future, directly contravening the aesthetic order. Amid that order: "The passage of time is the journey of the world towards the gathering of new ideas into actual fact" (RM:159). To that end practical traditions, as aesthetic undertakings, must cultivate the "habit of art," the habit of enjoying what Whitehead terms the "infinite variety of vivid values" (SMW:248–49).

As traditions cultivate that aesthetic habit, practical truths will be recreated as are the conditions under which their animating ideals achieve successive realizations. Traditions endure as the practical propositions they unfurl prove enticing and persuasive to successive enquirers. Yet while traditions effect their objective immortality through such distillations, they do so not first by recapitulating but by recreating their predecessors' achievements. According to Whitehead: "Every intellectual revolution which has ever stirred humanity into greatness has been a passionate protest against inert ideas" (AE:13).[10] Indeed he remarks: "Knowledge does not keep any better than fish," and in moral matters inert ideas are particularly harmful (AE:102). Here they signal lack of imagination and moral purposiveness, purposiveness properly rooted in an aesthetic order requiring perpetual reconstructions (AE:139–45). Traditions thus surrender their conceptual and practical integrity to the extent that they no longer induce novel realizations. Outworn traditions are falsified, however, less by their competitors than by the aesthetic order itself, from which they arose and to which they once—but no longer—lent vivid expression.

4

Perspectivism and Practical Truths

Whitehead's rejection of dogmatic methodologies suggests a progressive view of practical enquiry deeply at odds with MacIntyre's conservativism. Whitehead's account, however, more closely approximates to MacIntyre's own standards for successful rational enquiry, depicting more accurately how such enquiries progress, how they may identify and confront competitors, and how they might show themselves superior to rival enquiries. On MacIntyre's own terms, Whitehead's conception of practical enquiry more accurately depicts how rational traditions unfold and how they validate their truth claims.

Whitehead would agree with MacIntyre that rational enquiries embody teleologies and histories through which they select the evidences authoritative to them. Still, each method's selectivity implies that its achievements, if overextended, will distort the partial truths they might harbor by seeking to render them absolute or complete. Dogmatic recourse to such methods leads enquirers to ignore potential evidence beyond their investigations' scope, and falsifies those methods' deliverances if such partial analyses are mistaken for complete analyses. This methodological recourse also closes enquiries to substantive challenge, limiting their ability to advance. Such was the case, Whitehead's account would suggest, with Enlightenment theorists who rejected the general stock of metaphysical ideas they inherited. Their apparent antagonism to those ideas does not signal their advance beyond medieval theorists' dogmatism. Rather it signifies their own dogmatic recourse, as evidenced by their insistence that scientific discourse extrude final causes, an insistence that wrongly divorced natural and moral science (FR:38–41, 46–48). That split, rendering some modes of philosophy and science mutually unintelligible—incommensurable, in MacIntyre's language—

resulted not from discordant medieval and Enlightenment methodologies, but from their joint refusal to recognize their methods as delivering partial truths, and so from their refusal to seek more inclusive methods.

This refusal is also exemplified by MacIntyre, who rejects the possibility that seemingly incommensurable methods might prove complementary rather than logically incompatible. MacIntyre evinces this rejection through the notions of untranslatability and incommensurability he develops, and in the stark contrasts he draws between modern and premodern traditions. He argues, for example, that truth claims are so localized to traditions that much of their content cannot be translated. Moreover, he alleges that claims inhabiting premodern traditions bear strong truth conceptions that modern traditions preclude. He concludes that translations of premodern traditions' central texts inevitably distort those texts' meaning (WJ:386).

Whitehead's account, in contrast, premised upon the enduring allure of the ideals traditions embody, suggests that translation serves many functions. It not only reproduces but also recreates previously espoused truths, re-animating them in the present and for the future. Novel interpretations of the ideals and truths translation makes available proliferate as those ideals acquire added shading and content, and as their cognate conceptions of truth and rationality evolve. This process suggests both that the past remains past, that it is localized in ideals and truths that cannot be rendered present to contemporary enquirers in toto, and that those past ideals and truths may nonetheless be reenacted and absorbed into novel syntheses. Those truths' and ideals' partial translatability, then, implies both their importability into new contexts, and their ineradicable localization within particular traditions.

Whitehead's account would grant that contemporary translations render neither historical texts nor the cultural facts they incarnate wholly translucent. Yet contemporary difficulties translating and interpreting Aristotle's works, for example, would then indicate a condition of tradition-based enquiry, rather than, as MacIntyre claims, a defect marking contemporary enquiries alone (WJ:375). Moreover, even if one interpretation proved consistent with a text's original meaning, such consistency does not preclude the utility of other interpretations even in communicating that tradition's original content. Contemporary interpretations of Aristotle's political writings, for example, often emphasize as he did not potential conflicts between political power and rational authority. Amid such enquiries, to interpret Aristotle's works having accurate representation as one's sole goal risks distortions of its own, among them the prospect that truths thus localized might lose their force to solicit present enquirers' interest and response as they preclude or ignore those enquirers' contemporary concerns.

Additionally, while the view that all elements of a tradition are translatable might represent a modern conceit, MacIntyre's insistence that premodern texts' univocal authority prevents their substantive translation expresses an even older conceit: the conceit of the dogmatist. Against that view Whitehead's account suggests that granting those texts such authority ensnares MacIntyre in two fallacies: the misplaced concreteness and simple localization he flirts with in asserting that one tradition alone supplies the conditions of rational enquiry. Isolating premodern traditions from their modern counterparts, insisting upon their resources' untranslatability and incommensurability, negates their potential to engage contemporary debate, distorting their relation both to past and to future enquiry. Texts have multiple functions: to embody the past, to revivify the present, to direct the future—functions implying both their partial translatability and their partial untranslatability.

That triadic character, which MacIntyre's account both denies and presupposes, underscores how traditions retain their irreducibility within a broader practical inheritance that conjoins traditions' local particularities to their role as living exemplars. Traditions sustain their conceptual distance from each other through their untranslatability; they sustain their proximity through the broadly universal and broadly negotiable ideals they coin. Their dual functionality implies both the localization and the nonlocalization of their truth claims, and so implies the residence of particular traditions within a broader practical inheritance. An organic conception of that inheritance underlies Whitehead's claim that:

> History can only be understood by seeing it as the theater of diverse groups of idealists respectively urging ideals incompatible for conjoint realization. You cannot form any historical judgment of right or wrong by considering each group separately. (AI:356–57)

History can only be thus understood because the ideals these traditions develop and sustain, while localized, refer beyond their originating contexts. The incommensurable disputes practical traditions foster expose a common core: "The discordance over moral codes witnesses to the fact of moral experience. You cannot quarrel about unknown elements. The basis of every discord is some common experience, discordantly realized" (FR:69).

Tradition and Genealogy

MacIntyre denies that traditions evince such shared inheritances, insisting that contemporary disputes are interminable because they enact disputes among incommensurable traditions. Yet his position presupposes that the appropriate standard of truth for practical claims is that they secure dogmatic finality; that moral disputes admit wholesale rational resolution as a condition of moral agency; and that the historical processes that came to challenge these presumptions signify a disastrous wrong turn. These positions, however, place a faith in reason that borders on unreason, a faith that entails rejecting masses of evidence to the contrary. Indeed, even his own genealogy implies not univocal rational progress halted, but a succession of traditions securing partial and transitory achievements.

On MacIntyre's account the history Whitehead regards as continuous would exhibit a rupture between a premodern, well-ordered tradition and a modern disordered tradition, the latter rejecting the teleological and tradition-authoritative modes of enquiry that alone secure practical truth. Thus rending the history of rational enquiry, however, precludes those broader methods by which, MacIntyre's account implies, rational progress in practical enquiry is achieved. More starkly, that division militates against the practical achievements MacIntyre so admires, denying for example the methodological basis driving the Thomist synthesis, aiming as the latter did to afford greater conceptual adequacy than did its predecessors.

According to MacIntyre, Aquinas' synthesis retained the best elements of the Aristotelean and Augustinean traditions he inherited by rendering them mutually coherent. Yet that procedure presupposes a point MacIntyre rejects: that practical truths can inhabit multiple traditions. Moreover, Aquinas' approach effects the same method Whitehead adopts: reconceiving the common objects of the enquiry he inherited — God, teleology, truth — in the manner most amenable to those inheritances. This view of practical enquiry as integrative and systematic craft

Whitehead shares with Aquinas, but MacIntyre shares with neither, insisting as he does that practical enquiry proceeds by vanquishing rival formulations.

Moreover, he also rejects Whitehead's insight that even ostensibly rival traditions evolve jointly, a condition apart from which MacIntyre's own genealogy would founder. On MacIntyre's account, for example, practical enquiry exhibits a basic continuity from Aristotle to Hume, as they retain certain moral and social suppositions which reconcile individual and communal goods. In contrast, he identifies a breech between Aristotle and those moderns, particularly Kant, who deny those suppositions, a breech premised upon the latters' refusal of tradition-based enquiry. In rejecting reason in favor of emotion as the primary source of moral assessment, however, Hume presents a deeper discontinuity than does Kant with the Aristotelian tradition. Like Aristotle, Kant proposes a teleological vindication of reason's moral possibilities, possibilities Hume sharply restricts. For MacIntyre, that difference is less central to the relation between Hume and Aristotle than is their shared understanding of a moral community whose members ends' remain integrated (WJ:217, 293). The continuity between Aristotle and Hume, he suggests, is greater than that between Aristotle and Kant because the former retain the view that individual ends are to be socially resolved. Yet Kant aimed at a similar kind of community, though he thought its normative conditions were rationally constructed rather than naturally given. Moreover, like Aristotle, Kant aimed not to suggest a novel conception of moral judgment, but to systematize the moral principles he inherited.

Indeed, it is not their projects that differ so much as the mechanisms by which they vindicate their practical claims. Aristotle perpetuates a practical method premised upon a triadic faculty psychology—comprising reason, spirit or emotion, and passion—notoriously ambiguous on how these faculties interrelate apart from the latter's subordination to reason, which is presupposed. Subsequent investigations into that understanding of human nature took several forms: Aquinas thematizing natural reason, Augustine the will, Hume emotion, and Kant pure practical reason. These approaches propose quite different accounts, for example, of the relation between reason and emotion. Yet a shared inheritance underlies their confrontations, confrontations that repeatedly reopened fundamental assumptions for evaluation.

Kant's account of moral judgment, for example, admits into the practical sphere empirical, emotional elements he wished to exclude. He saw those elements as inadmissible because they resided in the natural or determined sphere, rather than in the autonomous sphere he believed human agency presupposes. Overlain upon that difficulty, he inherited from Aristotle a faculty psychology in which reason reigned supreme, subordinating emotion and passion. These inheritances complicated Kant's teleological project, as is evident in his positing of a 'feeling' of respect and of a 'natural human inclination' toward morality, concepts incompatible with the bifurcation of reason and nature he espouses. Despite the challenge his understanding of human nature presents to pure practical reason, however, Kant's project thematizes how reason becomes morally efficacious. Never challenged in this process is the Aristotelean assumption that reason itself is morally authoritative, is the principal identifier of moral goods and the final authority in moral judgments.

Thereby, Kant takes over from Aristotle an arché identifying reason as uniquely morally normative, and with it certain presumptions about reason's normative function. For Aristotle reason accrues moral authority because it is humans' distinctive function; yet nowhere does he show how that status alone renders reason uniquely morally normative. For Kant the primary practical question is not whether reason is the ultimate moral arbiter, but how it discharges this task apart from agents' other motivational tendencies. For that reason, however, the functional concepts and the a priori concepts their respective theories employ deny the potential normativity of other motive sources, falsely concealing the extent to which practical rationality might admit of multiple formulations according to multiple teleologies.

Both Aristotle and Kant, more specifically, adopt faculty psychologies now discredited both scientifically and metaphysically. Empirically,the alleged isolability of reason from emotional, biological, and social processes that these psychologies presuppose has been thoroughly undermined. Many investigators maintain the contrary position: reason is a function of these processes, not their master. Moreover, as Whitehead's account suggests, these processes incarnate norms conducing agents toward particular ends. That point does not invalidate the claim that particular reasoning patterns resolve these ends with variable efficacy. Yet it does deny that any particular instantiation of reason is uniquely morally normative in specifying such ends. The assumption that one such normative order is uniquely morally normative underlies those traditions MacIntyre avers as univocally patterning human goods. Apart from that dubious presupposition, however, none of these traditions shows how moral authority accrues to its norms such that all other possible norms must give way.

Even MacIntyre, for example, grants that emotions, desires, and preferences can express evaluative positions. Nevertheless he insists, these responses presuppose moralities (WJ:77). To insist that those responses presuppose moralities, however, submerges the coeval extent to which moralities presuppose the normative patterns—biological, emotional, social—they inhabit. Neither the moralities conditioning those responses nor the responses conditioning those moralities are independent variables; nor is either unilaterally authoritative. Moralities create and are created by such responses, as are instantiations of practical reason per se. The latter is no more fully autonomous from those elements than are those elements fully autonomous from reason.

Moreover, those elements harbor intentionalities distinct from reason's intentionalities. Did they not, practical rationality would be a given rather than a tenuous—and contentious—achievement. As it is not thus given, theories of practical rationality such as Aristotle's and Kant's are gravely concerned with securing reason's normative authority vis-à-vis other potential normative sources. Yet their theories specify a determinate set of human ends largely by fiat, begging the crucial question of how reason itself garners such authority. Still, that question remains at issue even in the consideration of why moral ends are held to properly restrict other ends. Even granting practical rationality the moral authority they propose, after all, why moral considerations should prove paramount in reconciling human means and ends remains at issue.

More specifically, both a priori and functional accounts posit intentional spheres of practical rationality; those accounts, however, do not necessarily underlie those spheres. The practical necessity their judgments deliver, Whitehead's account suggests, arise not from fixed, universal structures of human reason, but from intentional unities selected from broader normative sources and exhibiting an irreducible heteronomy of valuative sources. Questions concerning how reason becomes ethically efficacious, then, must precede the question of how a specific rational tradition assumes univocal normative force. To that extent, reason's authority may well derive itself from more primitive valuative processes guiding its construction. Any account of practical rationality, then, must defend not only the specific range of ideals it realizes, and the means by which it selects them, but also its rationale for regarding practical reasoning as morally normative.

Accordingly, MacIntyre's account goes only part way in acknowledging practical reason's situatedness. Practical rationalities, Whitehead's account suggests, are seeded by normative patterns rooted not only in historical traditions, but in biological, emotional, and social inheritances that both delimit and challenge reason's potential moral normativity. To that extent, those rationalities are constructed from multiple valuative sources never fully amenable to rational enclosure. Reason's practicality, then, is never merely given, but is constructed from antecedent processes that must be gathered into patterned coherencies. Those coherencies, the rival traditions MacIntyre depicts, confront challenge not only externally, not only from other traditions, but internally, as they only partially and precariously resolve the normative elements they comprise. For that reason, the conflict among rational traditions will tend not toward a final arche, but toward provisionally reconciling those pre-rational normative patterns to which reason's moral function is subject and from which that function arises.

Traditions: Past, Present, and Future

The unifying theme of Whitehead's more inclusive genealogy is twofold. First, it suggests that the divorce of practical conviction and rational justification that emotivism evinces is rooted not only in the conceptual disarray left in the Enlightenment's wake, but also in the Aristotelean assertion of reason's moral priority. That assertion denies the coevality of reason and of those emotional elements to which persuasion might appeal to secure moral conviction. Thereby, it dismisses the essentially persuasive function of those practical ideals and truths that secure such conviction. Second, the functional psychology underlying that assertion oversimplifies the teleological inheritances amid which practical enquiry works, positing as that teleology's driving factor what is in fact one of its most precarious achievements: practical reason.

Such simplification leads Aristotle's successors — Augustine, Aquinas, Kant, Hume — to develop more complex accounts of those countervailing motivational tendencies that Aristotle's functional psychology tenuously resolves. Yet to that extent the emotivist challenge arises not only from an Enlightenment-induced conceptual schizophrenia, but also from a schizophrenia embedded in those archi the Enlightenment inherits. The bifurcation MacIntyre identifies in the history of moral enquiry issues from dichotomies—reason versus power, reason versus emotion, reason versus persuasion—arising not from a rejection of traditional enquiries but as their logical consequence. Those traditions, affirming archi like those MacIntyre describes, intensify the conflict they aim to still, as they seek to establish as universally authoritative and morally binding norms that are in fact limited achievements. When those claims are not recognized as thus limited, the enquiries they inhabit become all the more tenuous, as they are then oriented not outward toward more inclusive methods, but inward toward exclusive reliance on their own limited resources.

Those enquiries' achievements, however, even if the products of finite traditions, would not on Whitehead's account be wholly undone. Indeed the folding in of such traditions upon themselves would signify their consummation, the determinancy and perfection of the ideals they incarnate as their bids for objective immortality. The perfections thus achieved, however, accrue not to the traditions but to the enduring ideals and methods they distill—which alone persist. Still, those enduring ideals militate against closed conceptions of tradition. In embodying their distinctive truths and ideals, traditions realize enduring archetypes or styles of normative practice that persist to the extent that they afford persuasive possibilities to successive adherents. Thereby, the ideals and truths traditions spawn inhabit not logically incompatible projects, but a partially shared practical project admitting multiple developments—a shared tradition of practical inheritances.

Such an inheritance, harboring multiple practical possibilities neither wholly logically compatible nor incompatible, would admit not of a closed arche but of multiple archai unfolding vis-à-vis each other. At the same time, positing such a broad-based tradition contravenes one of MacIntyre's central assumptions: that traditions are well-ordered only when they preclude substantive disagreement. Such a view is oddly out of place in MacIntyre's otherwise highly contextualized conception of practical truth, a conception premised upon faith in dogmatic tradition. Moreover, it undercuts his recognition that practical enquiries must admit contingencies into their rational fabrics. On his account, those particularities ensure that traditions remain incommensurable, incapable of rationally confronting each other. Such an account, however, thus begs the underlying question: the extent to which traditions are rationally constituted at all.

For MacIntyre, the latter question could not be posed apart from a particular tradition, because any answer would then presuppose a standard of rationality independent of any tradition. Yet even granting the impossibility of such a standard, a perspectivism like that White-head's account implies affords rational standards independent of any particular tradition without thereby claiming independence of tradition per se. MacIntyre would reject that proposal on several grounds: (1) its open arche would not render truth and tradition coeval, (2) the multiple norms sustaining that arche would adduce constructed as well as given or discovered normative orders, and (3) those orders would inevitably conflict. A Whiteheadian account of practical enquiry would not, however, dissolve the link between practical traditions and practical truths. It would merely acknowledge traditions' dual function in discovering and recreating those truths, granting that function an essentially futural orientation.

Moreover, that understanding of enquiry would embody a different stance toward moral conflict. According to MacIntyre, our "interminable" moral conflicts signal a disordered tradition wherein "survivals" from past traditions linger incoherently, bereft of their legitimating contexts. On a Whiteheadian account, in contrast, such survivals would represent transtraditional ideals that must be attached to and reanimated by present realities if they are to retain their persuasive force. That effort at revivification would eschew MacIntyre's adversial approach, his emphasis upon conflict among "rival" and "alien" traditions. For MacIntyre such an approach alone permits traditions to prove their rational hegemony (WJ:334). MacIntyre's account, however, denies those shared inheritances and common endeavors through which traditions might become rivals or conspirators; hence it denies the possibility of constructive debate among them. In contrast, a Whiteheadian perspectivism would permit substantive debate, admitting even the survivals whose fate MacIntyre mourns not as unintelligible holdovers, but as ideals that might be reanimated.

Those admissions, however, require also accepting that progressive traditions conjoin past and future not merely via reiteration but also by recreation and by creation. They require agents to conjoin anew the given and inherited and created practical resources through which substantive truths evolve as enquiry advances. Such an account is antithetical to the closed arche and the constricted range of practical rationality MacIntyre advocates. He claims, for example, that a tradition's arche must be sustained to specify the determinate standards by which any practical enquiry can measure its rational progress toward 'final adequacy' (WJ:47). Yet that progress, he grants, can only be maintained by suppressing disruptive elements, as he admits was necessary to sustain the Thomist synthesis (WJ:183–208). On a Whiteheadian account, in contrast, such recourse would be the inevitable issue of a tradition that had lost its persuasive capacity and rational authority, and so could be sustained only by force.

Tradition and Adventure

According to Whitehead, the undeniable residence of traditions within historical matrices should not blind us to an equally important truth: "the definition of culture as the knowledge of the best that has been said and done . . . omits the great fact that in their day the great achievements of the past were the adventures of the past" (AI:360). Indeed he claims: "It is a curious delusion that the rock upon which our beliefs can be founded is an historical investigation. You can only interpret the past in terms of the present . . . history presupposes a metaphysic" (RM:84). That metaphysic discloses that while our practical enquiries may be bound to their particular origins, they nevertheless aspire to universality; while they may be bound to particular historical instantiations, they aspire to enduring truth.

Those aspirations, Whitehead maintains, animate the religious and teleological enquiries wherein rationalism takes flight. That rationalism, embodied in its practical and speculative incarnations, holds out the following operative ideal: "That we fail to find in experience any elements intrinsically incapable of exhibition as examples of general theory is the hope of rationalism" (PR:42). Such hope can take form in multiple enquiries, including those enquiries embedded in dogmatic religious traditions. Any such enquiry, however, admits strict limits to its utility when it suppresses enquiry: "But if the same dogma be used intolerantly so as to check the employment of other modes of analyzing the subject matter, then, for all its truth, it will be doing the work of falsehood" (RM:131). Work on the part of falsehood is particularly evident among those traditions that restrict speculative freedom and refuse to admit novel conceptual resources. That refusal is inimical even to well-ordered religious traditions that properly aim to interpret universal experiences and so must continually amplify, recast, and generalize their ideas "so as to absorb into one system all sources of experience" (RM:149). Indeed, Whitehead claims, such efforts animate religious enquiry: "Religion is the translation of general ideas into particular thoughts, particular emotions, and particular purposes; it is directed to the end of stretching individual interest beyond its self-defeating particularity" (PR:15).

That extension beyond self-defeating particularity, he maintains, requires those enquiries to continuously advance "in proportion of truth" (RM:149). Growth eludes those enquiries that become shut up in "their own forms of thought, unfertilized and self-satisfied" (RM:147). Such enquiries fail at their chief task: "The task of reason is to fathom the deeper depths of the many-sidedness of things" (PR:342). Moreover, they fail to adequately investigate their most important objects:

> The chief danger to philosophy is narrowness in the selection of evidence. This narrowness arises from the idiosyncrasies and timidities of particular authors, of particular social groups, of particular schools of thought, of particular epochs in the history of civilization. The evidence is arbitrarily biased by the temperaments of individuals, by the provincialities of groups, and by the limitations of schemes of thought. The evil, resulting from this distortion of evidence, is at its worst in the consideration . . . of ultimate ideals. (PR:337)

The evil Whitehead envisions here is all the worse because it undercuts our enquiries into the teleologies we inhabit, and in particular religious enquiries. According to Whitehead:

> Religion is an ultimate craving to infuse into the insistent particularity of emotion that non-temporal generality which primarily belongs to conceptual thought alone. . . . The two sides of the organism require a reconciliation in which emotional experiences illustrate a conceptual justification, and conceptual experiences find an emotional illustration. (PR:16)

Such an account recognizes the ineliminable locality both of practical judgments and of the truth conditions sustaining them. For Whitehead: "all judgment is categorical; it concerns a proposition true or false in its application to the actual occasion which is the subject making the judgment" (PR:200). At the same time every proposition refers to a universe exhibiting a metaphysical character. While every proposition accords to that character, however: "A proposition can embody partial truth because it only demands a certain type of systematic environment, which is presupposed in its meaning. It does not refer to the universe in all its detail" (PR:11).

Partial, even incompatible truths can coexist provided they do not arrogate to themselves univocal authority. According to MacIntyre, practical truths coexist only within a univocal, tradition-constituted rational framework. For Whitehead, in contrast, that demand would negate the conditions under which those truths are both constructed and discovered, and whose provisionality delimits their truth-accruing potential. Traditions are thus irretrievably open not because they confront rivals, but because they construct distinct normative domains from partially shared sources. Those sources, in turn, are available transtraditionally as well as locally, and endure insofar as they link their local practical concerns to transtraditional resources and challenges.

While traditions condition the norms sustaining their animating ideals, the latter's specificity engenders the conflicts among practical truths that will be their undoing. Such conflicts betray those propositions as finite selections whose persuasive potential may well diminish. According to MacIntyre, such diminution would signal those propositions' "rational defeat." Conversely, on Whitehead's account, regarding such conflict as effecting practical propositions' wholesale rational defeat presupposes conditions inimical to practical enquiry's progress:

> So long as the dogmatic fallacy infects the world, this discordance will continue to be misinterpreted. . . . But as soon as the true function of rationalism is understood, that it is a gradual approach to ideas of clarity and generality, the discord is what may be expected. (FR:71)

This dogmatic fallacy is fatal to rational progress because it misrepresents how propositions function in rational enquiry:

> The conception of propositions as merely material for [logical] judgments is fatal to any understanding of their role in the universe. In that purely logical aspect, non-conformal propositions are merely wrong, and therefore worse than useless. But in their primary role, they pave the way along which the world advances into novelty. Error is the price we pay for progress. (PR:187)

Here, Whitehead does not advocate progress for the sake of progress, any more than he advocates rejecting past achievements for the sake of rejecting past achievements. Rather, he takes as the main challenge of his metaphysical enquiry the effort to render coherent the historical passage of ideals: "The world is thus faced by the paradox that, at least in its higher actualities, it craves for novelty and yet is haunted by terror at the loss of the past . . . the culminating fact of conscious, rational life refuses to conceive itself as a transient enjoyment, transiently useful" (PR:340). Indeed he maintains: "The most general formulation of the religious problem is the question whether the process of the temporal world passes into the formation of other actualities, bound together in an order in which novelty does not mean loss" (PR:340).

The world's realities are thus bound, he maintains, but only in part. The world and God are co-creators, and amid their ongoing creativity it is not actual facts that endure, but the conceptual lures that solicit such facts and may be thereby repeatedly revivified. Amid their passage, actualities secure objective immortality only by transmitting their achievements to God's Consequent nature, which proposes those ideals anew to the world's subsequent incarnations. Thereby God: "transmutes what has been lost into a living fact within His own nature. . . . In its union with God that fact is not a total loss, but on its finer side is an element to be woven immortally into the rhythm of mortal things" (RM:155). Each living fact, however, requires realization anew, and risks loss of vividness and immediacy if it fails as an objective lure: "It decays by transmitting its nature to slighter occasions of actuality, by reason of the failure of the new forms to fertilize the perspective achievements which constitute its past history" (RM:160).

That passage, Whitehead maintains, is inevitable because all achievements embody finite selections from a broader array of possibilities, not all of which may be revivified. Indeed, he maintains, the order this passage exemplifies will itself pass away: "The present type of order in the world has arisen from an unimaginable past, and its future will find its grave in an unimaginable future" (RM:160). For that reason, our enquiries into such matters neither secure univocal nor eternal truths, nor propose wholly determinate normative standards fixed for all time. We may aim to formulate such practical truths and standards, but they will neither endure nor be realized truthfully if they contravene the broader teleology delimiting their scope and utility. That utility itself is not embodied in particular formulas, but in their enduring potential beyond their original formulations:

The formula sinks in importance, or even is abandoned; but its meaning remains fructifying in the world, finding new expression to suit new circumstances. The formula was not wrong, but it was limited to its own sphere of thought. (RM:136)

5

Whitehead's Aesthetic Teleology

The previous analyses suggest that on the central points driving MacIntyre's restorative project, Whitehead's positions are superior to MacIntyre's on the latter's own terms. Whitehead's view of tradition is more inclusive of its inheritances than is MacIntyre's. Moreover, Whitehead's commitment to metaphysical adequacy sustains substantive continuity among those inheritances, approximating better to the narrative model of truth discovery and justification that MacIntyre proposes. Whitehead would deny MacIntyre's insistence that a univocal narrative authoritatively guides speculative and practical reason. Yet his refusal would issue from a view of practical enquiry more consonant with the traditions we inherit and more adequate to the resources those traditions make available than is MacIntyre's. Still, Whitehead's teleology faces three challenges from the outset: (1) the role of God within his system, (2) his account of moral agency, and (3) the apparent difficulty his aesthetic teleology has in supplying determinate criteria for practical evaluation. These issues must be addressed here because Whitehead never developed the implications his system has for practical enquiry, a lack some critics falsely attribute to his metaphysics' inability to support such developments.[1]

The criticisms Whitehead's teleology confronts are interrelated. Whitehead's theological references, some claim, assign God ad hoc the task of tying up his system's loose ends, a task He cannot perform because His nature as Whitehead describes it presents an exception to some of his system's first principles.[2] In contrast, others charge that while consonant with those first principles, Whitehead's God plays so determinative a role in the self-constitutions of actualities that it compromises the freedom their agency presupposes.[3] Still other critics argue that God's role is so diffuse, so indeterminate in specifying a distinctive normative order, that it offers no substantive criteria for practical assessment. Indeed, such critics charge, Whitehead's system harbors no such criteria.[4]

The first charge, that the God Whitehead describes either contravenes his system's first metaphysical principles, or functions too determinatively to permit the agency he ascribes even to barely organic actualities, has spawned immense debate among Whitehead followers and critics alike. That debate is vast, but its central directions are animated respectively by (*a*) those who grant that Whitehead's God is systematically untenable, yet maintain that the system need not posit such an entity to preserve its coherence, and (*b*) those who maintain that God's role is necessary to and consistent with the system, and who variously depict that consistency.[5]

The latter position is fully consonant with the letter and the spirit of Whitehead's cosmology, as he was committed to a teleology bearing essential theological reference. That teleology portrays God as supplying actualities their initial subjective aims, as primordially evaluating the ideal potentials those aims entertain, and as securing the objective immortality through which actualities effect their influence beyond their subjective immediacy. Thereby God sustains continuity among actualities, guiding their inheritances from their initial valuations, to their satisfactions, to their "superjective" expanses into the future. Directing that continuity are God's aesthetic ends, eliciting actualities both individually and collectively to pursue their aims in accordance with His. God thus supplies the normative framework that evokes complex feeling patterns, including emotion, mentality, and practical and speculative reason.

While God seeds these processes, Whitehead stresses that their results do not come to fruition until individuals render their decisions upon His valuations. God does not lay down wholly determinate norms but supplies lures for feeling, persuading individuals but not dictating their decisions. Moreover, God's nature is incomplete without those decisions, which effect His subsequent valuations. The mutually adjusting decisions of God and of the world wash over each other in successive waves. God requires the world no less than the world requires God, as God is affected by the world's activities. Accordingly, to isolate God as the sole creative force within Whitehead's teleology is to deny His Consequent nature, which shepherds into itself the decisions the world effects as components of His determinancy.

In these ways God exemplifies the conditions every actual entity labors under. He is creative and patient, inheriting a set of valuations from which His persuasive task proceeds and to which it recurs in evoking subsequent decisions. Moreover, like any actual entity, He manages His inheritances to conform with His ends, omitting from His Consequent nature those elements inconsistent with His efforts to bring forth intense, novel, harmonious experience. His Consequent nature thus refuses to admit those decisions regarded as thwarting valuative potential or as encouraging no valuative potential beyond themselves, those decisions thus identified as embodying "evil." The latter decisions, Whitehead maintains, are as real as any others. Yet they surrender their potential for objective immortality, for representation in God's Consequent nature, by refusing to conform to the normative order God incarnates: "The consequent nature of God is His judgment upon the world. He saves the world as it passes into the immediacy of His own life. It loses nothing . . . that can be saved" (PR:346).

While Whitehead's depiction of God's nature thereby accounts for the reality of evil and for its passage, the theodicy he proposes raises the objection all theodicies raise: that it falsifies the effects of evil, which endure. Some critics take that endurance as reason enough to suggest that Whitehead posits his God not only to unify his metaphysical first principles, but to render coherent with them an intractable contingency riddling human experience: the possibility that evil might triumph over good.[6] Despite that issue's complexities, however, the central dispute remains between those who maintain that God is a consistent element of Whitehead's system and those who maintain that He is not. Both positions, however, afford partial truths. Those who grant God's role as Whitehead describes it reaffirm Whitehead's claim that the intuition of world order underlying reason's unfolding is essentially religious. Those who deny God's necessity, in contrast, can do so without denying that God remains a possible theological referent. Whitehead himself opens up this possibility:

> The secularization of the concept of God's functions in the world is at least as urgent a requisite of thought as the secularization of other elements in experience. The concept of God is certainly one essential element in religious feeling. But the converse is not true; the concept of religious feeling is not an essential element in the concept of God's function in

the universe. In this respect religious literature has been sadly misleading to philosophic theory, partly by attraction and partly by repulsion. (PR:207)

On this count both theists and nontheists can find a home in Whitehead's system. While the theists could retain the theological positions Whitehead proposes, the nontheists could maintain with equal plausibility that God's functions can be taken over by other elements within the system. God's Primordial and Consequent functions could be taken over by the past and future conceived as routes of inheritance, and His superjective aspect could be devolved to actual entities, whose collective activities could lay down norms seeding aesthetic and moral orders. The proposal that God is a possible but not necessary part of Whitehead's system would diverge from his position most basically in rendering complex actualities more tenuous, more contingent, and more transitory than Whitehead allows. Yet that difference would signify disparate interpretive and observational emphases, not disagreement over first principles.

At the same time, that proposal has several implications for the conceptions of practical rationality and of agency that Whitehead's system supports. Traditional teleologies, like Aristotle's, set forth a determinate conception of human nature that limned ideals of character and conduct and thereby circumscribed agents' obligations. Whitehead's teleology is not thus determinative. Indeed, so complex are its normative processes that some critics maintain Whitehead cannot even account for enduring self-identities, much less for moral agency.[7] Such critics take issue with Whitehead's intensely naturalistic account of personal orders, arguing that even if the processes he describes explain complex natural phenomena, they do not account for the subjective intensity and agency defining human experience. Rendering human experience continuous with amoeba or plant experience, explaining those experiences' disparities as differences of degree rather than kind, strains credulity. Human agents, such critics suggest, are self-aware and self-directing and self-responsible, capacities too complex to be accounted for merely by routes of patterned emotional inheritances among actualities.[8]

These objections, however, arise largely from two assumptions which Whitehead takes to task: (1) that the rational, conscious self is the locus of human agency, and (2) that that locus' continuity is substantially given. Such assumptions exemplify the fallacies of misplaced concreteness and simple location. Whitehead claims of our sense of enduring self-identity, for example, that that sense misleads us if we mistake it to found that identity.[9] This identity, rather, results from massive emotional inheritances the vast bulk of which we are never consciously aware. The sense of an enduring self is abstracted from that matrix of inheritances, a selective emphasis that falsifies those inheritances if taken as their cause rather than their consequence. That enduring inheritance, moreover, is localized amid an organic body and thus substantially continuous with its environs despite its apparent discontinuity with that environment—its immediate self-presence.

That personal presence, rather, signifies a surface phenomenon attending the deeply impersonal processes—emotional, biological, social—forging it. Those processes condition that presence's recreations, reeffecting the intimately familiar, intimately personal patterns falsely identified as sturdy givens rather than as precarious achievements. Prepersonal as those processes are, however, they are not for that reason non-normative. Rather, they lay down protonormative inheritances amid which the distinctive biological, emotional, and social patternings marking human agency and accountability arise. The personal identities agents subsequently construct will thus admit norms largely autonomous of rational control; indeed, that control will be their issue.[10] These prepersonal processes, then, rooted in actualities' physical inheritances, conceptual appetitions, and satisfactions, become increasingly varied and interiorized, evoking, remodulating, and constructing autonomous normative patterns of their own, among them the subjectivity and intense novel conceptuality evinced for example when persons come to entertain moral ideals.[11]

Those constructive processes underlie both the aesthetic order Whitehead's account details and the normative orders it spawns, including that order wherein human agency and moral accountability arise. These orders, both discovered and created, accord to that teleology's aesthetic mandates, which induce intense, novel, harmonious valuative experiences. That conformity fosters the growth of conceptual potential, of actualities' ability to entertain options, to entertain potential ends, and to realize values. This capacity is always present in germ, yet is never wholly determinative, nor are the patterned orders that givenness both implies and presupposes. Granted that some order is given, particular normative orders embody permutations of that givenness, instantiating thereby their own distinctive norms.

Those orders are precarious achievements, enduring perhaps, but neither eternal nor isolable from their temporal instantiations. Such orders neither yield nor are yielded by Aristotelean substances, the fixed natures often alleged to underlie the personal identities we affirm, the characters we identify, the functional concepts of human nature we hold out as moral ideals. Ideal patterns, exemplars, may endure. But to hold out personal identity, or character, or human nature as evincing univocal moral norms is to misconstrue the processes that shape them. Human nature, for example, cannot be considered a univocally authoritative source from which timeless normative premises can be unilaterally abstracted. Rather, sundry normative patterns subsist under the title human nature, all inhabiting the amorphous processes from which particular exemplary patterns are constructed.

Human nature thus comprises not a singular exemplary pattern given by God or nature or reason or convention, but multiple normative patterns constructed and reconstructed amid the aesthetic order Whitehead depicts. Such exemplars present themselves as relatively enduring patterns of activity—of disposition, culture, character, practice, attention and reasoning, genetic tendency, even—but not as wholly normatively determinative entities in their own right. The claim, then, that a particular conception of human nature determines once and for all human ends and possibilities, sets forth univocal norms for moral valuation and practical reasoning, gets its analysis backwards. Each such exemplar comprises multiple inheritances, multiple ends, multiple norms to which that alleged nature does not give rise, but from which it issues. That nature is thus subject to norms that its constructive agency can manage, direct, and modulate—but never wholly rationalize. Human natures qua moral ideals, then, signify not given sources of practical enquiries, but those enquiries' enduring products.

Matters Metaphysical

The charge that Whitehead's teleology supplies determinate bases neither for practical enquiry nor for human agency is both accurate and misleading. The norms he describes offer evaluative standards neither wholly given and discoverable as strict realists would have us believe, nor wholly invented as strict constructivists would have us believe. Those standards, rather, are constructed amid normative patterns over which agents at best effect partial, precarious, and indeterminate control. No normative hierarchy univocally resolves the ends appropriate to such agents. Those ends, rather, are variously hierarchized through normative patterns spawning multiple practical ideals that themselves serve ends beyond the morally normative ends they present.

That absence of a given hierarchy of ends is a condition of moral agency, not its refutation. Moral norms are products and processes of abstraction, of the selective emphases by which agents select their activities' means and ends. The aesthetic teleology Whitehead proposes conditions these decisions and the norms they effect. Yet those conditions do not unilaterally specify which norms will be realized or which ideals incarnated. Rather, those specifications are selected and reaffirmed by the actualities reconstructing them. These selections, however, mobilize vast conceptual resources, the flashes of novel appetition permitting complex actualities' constituents to entertain ever wider valuative options that may or may not reproduce the complexes' constitutive patterns. Still, complex endurances evince through their expanded valuative potential the singular advantage of relative abstraction from the normative patterns constructing them, evince greater capacity to autonomously reconstruct themselves amid those processes.

That abstractive potential issues from the selectivity complexes' constituents effect, which permits endurances to inaugurate novel normative patterns—biological, emotional, social—soliciting novel conceptual realizations, novel valuations. The norms thus built channel, reproduce, and intensify actualities' potential for novel satisfactions. Thereby those norms foster the conditions under which freedom, agency, selectivity among ends, including moral selectivity, become efficacious. To that extent freedom signifies the mutual limitations of norms and the actualities selecting and incarnating them. Those limitations are thus constructed by valuative processes that cannot be wholly rationalized. Yet they can be made intelligible as they elicit the norms built and reappropriated through individual and collective choice.

Those choices will be restricted by the partly given, partly constructed conditions sustaining them. Yet those conditions spawn many possible abstractions from the givens they admit, and so lead agents to reconstruct those givens. Accordingly, for example, Aristotle's account of appropriate human means and ends comes to be supplemented historically by accounts bearing counterabstractions, counterselective emphases through which will and emotion and pure practical reason specify the

moral life's operative intentionality. Importantly, though, such intentionalities become operative not only in discovering appropriate means and
ends but in constructing a morally normative sphere whose means and
ends admit of substantive choice.

This account suggests that while we occupy no neutral starting
point from which to assess our selective emphases, the traditions we
inherit, we do countenance shared normative inheritances from which
we can abstract sufficiently to evaluate their relative merits. We can do so
because traditions' norms are neither simply given, by nature or God or
history, nor constructive of the practical enquiries they evoke. Rather,
those enquiries follow upon the norms they thematize and reconstruct.
Those reconstructions, moreover, realize norms and ideals that, however
enduring, do not accrue univocal normative force. They eschew such
force because the norms they propose serve also the aesthetic ends
Whitehead's teleology depicts, and so cannot afford the unique or self-
sufficient set of ends defining human agency. Rather, those norms themselves embody and serve wider ends.

That MacIntyre ignores these protonormative processes underscores the metaphysical inadequacy of his account of practical enquiry's
progress. More importantly, it infects both his diagnosis of the emotivists'
plight and his prescription for amending that plight. The roots of this
inadequacy are hinted at in *After Virtue*, in MacIntyre's effort to restore
Aristotle's teleological ethic while rejecting that ethic's metaphysical
basis. MacIntyre acknowledges that his project confronts several cogent
challenges: "The first of these concerns the way in which Aristotle's teleology presupposes his metaphysical biology. If we reject that biology, as
we must, is there any way in which that teleology can be preserved?"
(AV:152). Yet his own account, MacIntyre maintains, premised on
agents' practices, narratives, and traditions, requires no natural teleological grounding:

> It is—happily—not Aristotelian in two ways in which a good
> deal of the rest of the tradition also dissents from Aristotle.
> First, although this account of the virtues is teleological, it
> does not require any allegiance to Aristotle's metaphysical
> biology. And secondly, just because of the multiplicity of
> human practices and the consequent multiplicity of goods in
> the pursuit of which the virtues may be exercised—goods
> which will often be contingently incompatible and which will

therefore make rival claims upon our allegiance—conflict will not spring solely from flaws in individual character. (AV:183)

As conflict among rival goods does not spring from disordered characters, however, MacIntyre's account is at odds not only with Aristotle's teleology but also with the kind of teleology MacIntyre claims must obtain if agents are to pursue their activities rationally. Such a teleology requires a determinate hierarchy of ends and goods absent which agents cannot exercise practical judgment. Yet apart from a metaphysically grounded hierarchy, it is unclear how any particular hierarchy could accrue univocal normative force, could comprise agents' essential ends.

Those difficulties reverberate throughout *After Virtue*'s successor: *Whose Justice? Which Rationality?* MacIntyre undertook this second work, he says, because: "I also recognized that these conclusions required support from an account of what rationality is, in light of which rival and incompatible evaluations of the arguments of *After Virtue* could be adequately accounted for" (WJ:ix). Subsequent upon *After Virtue*, he affirms: "I promised a book in which I should attempt to say both what makes it rational to act in one way rather than another and what makes it rational to advance and defend one conception of practical rationality rather than another. Here it is" (WJ:ix).

MacIntyre's second effort, however, founders upon the same difficulties as the first. MacIntyre notes in this work's preface that "[d]ifferent and incompatible conceptions of justice are characteristically closely linked to different and incompatible conceptions of practical rationality" (WJ:ix). He traces these conceptions from their Aristotelean to their Enlightenment instantiations, purportedly disclosing a substantive break in their evolution signified by the modern elevation of individual over common interests. His genealogy, however, distorts the substantive continuity underlying the persistent reworking of Aristotle's ideal of justice, an ideal requiring that we treat equals equally. MacIntyre's own genealogy depicts the successive incarnations of that ideal: from Aristotle's identification of "natural" equals, through Aquinas' extension of that ideal to all Christians, to the Enlightenment's expansion of that ideal to include all rational agents.

More importantly, though, MacIntyre's genealogy underscores the difficulties his account confronts upon its rejection of Aristotle's metaphysical biology and the teleological determinacy it affords. For MacIntyre that biology has patently unacceptable implications for practical enquiry:

> What is likely to affront us—and rightly—is Aristotle's writing
> off of non-Greeks, barbarians and slaves, as not merely not pos-
> sessing political relationships, but as incapable of them. . . .
> Aristotle writes as if barbarians and Greeks had fixed natures
> and in so viewing them he brings home to us once again the
> ahistorical character of his understanding of human nature.
> (AV:149)

Apart from a fixed conception of human nature, however, it's unclear
how Aristotle could maintain his claim that human nature proposes univocally normative moral ends embodying a determinate hierarchy of
goods. MacIntyre's own conceptions of practical rationality and of justice, developed throughout *After Virtue* and *Whose Justice? Which Rationality?*, never accrue the determinate specificity necessary to show how
his conceptions are uniquely normative. *After Virtue* never specifies how
some practices may be judged superior to others, and *Whose Justice?
Which Rationality?* offers an extensive genealogy that militates against
the claim that a single conception of practical reason could be uniquely
normative.[12]

Aristotle inscribes his ideal of justice within a metaphysical cosmology that arbitrarily excludes potential agents from the polis, wherein
alone questions of justice arise. MacIntyre rejects this arbitrariness. Yet
those exclusions are underwritten by metaphysical principles circumscribing a human nature that embodies determinate practical principles
apart from which normative judgments could not be rationally rendered.
Moreover, to commend arbitrarily removing from Aristotle's cosmology
those elements that "affront" us contravenes both MacIntyre's claim that
tradition bears unique moral authority, and his suggestion that importing
modern concerns into premodern traditions illicitly vitiates their truth
claims.

For Aristotle, slaves are by nature barred from political participa-
tion. Yet MacIntyre does not engage the metaphysical principles, the
fixed natures, underlying this assertion; he merely rejects the assertion.
In addition, his subsequent affirmation of the Thomist cosmology arbitrarily exchanges one metaphysical system for another. This exchange
does not signal the rational unfolding practical enquiry requires. Rather,
it signifies his importation of Aristotle's virtue ethic into a Thomist cosmology espousing conceptions of justice and practical rationality at odds
with Aristotle's on metaphysical grounds. Given MacIntyre's insular view

of traditions, the Thomist universalization of justice and equality, premised upon a divine order, should represent an encroachment upon the Aristotelean tradition unintelligible in the latter's terms.

Moreover, the metaphysical inadequacy of MacIntyre's account is evident also in his adoption of Aristotle's functional psychology. According to MacIntyre, the contemporary diminution of rational moral authority underlies the rise of emotivism, which affirms that practical judgments embody preferences alone. Preferences, he maintains, cannot be rationally adjudicable because they "express only attitudes or feelings" (AV:11). In thus framing the emotivist challenge, MacIntyre reaffirms the traditional dichotomy between reason and emotion which represents emotion as a threat to reason's dominion. That dichotomy, exemplified by Aristotle as well as by most of his Enlightenment successors, enjoins the submission of emotional elements of motivation and judgment to their rational counterparts. As Whitehead's account suggests, however, that segregation assumes dubious metaphysical grounds, among them reason's isolability from the emotional, biological, and social processes attending it.

Segregating these processes from normative evaluation's provenance reenforces the modern bifurcation of facts and values that MacIntyre rejects and that emotivism presupposes. Conversely, Whitehead's account suggests that the segregation of reason and emotion MacIntyre presupposes divorces reason from the valuative processes that direct it toward its ends, circumscribing the intentional unities, the traditions harboring evaluative judgments. To bear objective normative force, Whitehead's account suggests, valuative judgments must comprise all motive and agent elements, whose conjunctions alone yield normative judgments both factual and evaluative. The preferences MacIntyre dismisses as subjective and thus as unsuitable grounds for normative evaluations on Whitehead's account exhibit essential objective references. As they bear both subjective and objective references, they prove rationally adjudicable, albeit not determinately.

On a Whiteheadian account, MacIntyre's position assumes falsely that preferences are not rationally adjudicable, excluding them from normative assessment. That exclusion, however, does not accurately depict preferences' potential evaluative function. Rather it flows from traditional efforts to frame a conception of practical rationality accruing a measure of evaluative determinacy, a measure of practical truth, which moral evaluation does not support. That endeavor animates the conception of practical enquiry as affording a moral science, a rational system of objective, timeless practical truths. Yet it reduplicates thereby the irrationality of those Enlightenment theorists who sought a degree of practical intelligibility unavailable to agents inhabiting an irremediably contingent world.

Attempts to extrude matters of taste and of preference from normative evaluation, on a Whiteheadian account, exemplify this irrationality. Such efforts signal the presumption that the intelligibility, justification, and motive force of practical claims require wholesale rational agreement among agents. To that end, practical norms for evaluating character and conduct that might sustain a univocal evaluative context would supersede aesthetic criteria envisioning multiple moral ideals. Yet aesthetic criteria underlie the moral norms traditions incarnate. As the latter elicit the emotional patternings by which moral norms become intelligible, motivational, and justified, they seed those traditions distilling ideals that evoke normative judgments. This point underscores the centrality of aesthetic criteria in assessing practical ideals, the traditions that bear them, and the characters and actions that realize them. Those criteria identify traditions and ideals as abstractions, possibilities selected from a broader array of potential normative orders. They also illustrate how traditions harbor and confront the irremediable contingencies precluding their claims to univocal normative authority.

Such authority is untenable, Whitehead's account suggests, because however well resolved, those contingencies restrict the extent to which practical rationalities autonomously specify human goods or ends, even morally normative goods or ends. Assuming practical rationalities unilaterally specify those ends invokes several fallacies. Practical rationalities embody multiple normative sources and variously sustain a range of normatively intelligibile patterns. To that extent, norms born of preferences and interests permit practical evaluations coeval with other norms and no less integral to agents' selections of means and ends. While retaining partial autonomy in specifying such goods, these norms will not contravene but will underwrite practical reason's evaluative patterns.

That last point is critical to understanding how practical rationalities unfold for three reasons. First, as they are rooted in protonorms, their deliverances are less determinate and more open to revision than accounts such as MacIntyre's suggest. Accordingly, the familiar denigration of emotional propensities as potentially morally normative can be reconsidered without invalidating the ideals animating previous enquiries. Instead, such enquiries can be seen as proposing norms inviting revision in light of, for example, contemporary neurobiological investigations that depict biological processes as playing a larger role in judicative activities than has previously been acknowledged.

Second, those protonorms suggest that while agency, character, and human nature represent enduring concepts guiding moral enquiry, they do not comprise closed archai valorizing particular patterns of human nature or character. Rather, those protonorms remain partly autonomous from the normative patterns constructed from them, ensuring a plurality of constructions. So, for example, the enduring patterns by which anger, or passion, or beneficence are integrated into human activities and incarnate practical ideals—Stoic, Epicurean, Aristotelean, Thomist, Kantian—will represent possible mechanisms for rendering those emotional patterns morally efficacious, for conducing them to serve human goods. Yet neither those ideals nor the goods they sanction will univocally delimit THE human good. Rather, those ends will embody patterns of practical activity and of practical rationality that present ideals referable to multiple normative sources among which moral goods are one class— but not the sole arbiters—of human goods.

Third, as morally normative criteria are not the sole arbiters of goods, nor even of human goods, but are themselves built and reconstructed from sources partly given and partly created, practical rationalities will be charged with creating as well as with discovering practical truths. Practical enquiries will harbor conflict and even interminable disputes not as a signal of their decay but as a function and condition of their progress. Such enquiries will incarnate distinctive archai, sets of first principles expressing their guiding ideals. Yet they will vindicate their ideals not first through their rational defense, but through their ability to make their coherence and fidelity to experience persuasive to potential adherents. Only then will their animating ideals assume the intelligibility, motive force, and justification marking well-ordered traditions.

Conversely, as their persuasiveness diminishes, practical ideals surrender their efficacy regardless of their rational appeal. They may be reborn, but the crucial truth test they face is again persuasiveness. Continual opposition fosters their evolution, apart from which they will not survive. Absent continual revivification they become inert ideas, enforcable by fiat or force but not through their own persuasiveness. And proportionate to such enforcement, they conduce to the emotivism and relativism that imperil all practical ideals. Such a defense imperils those ideals because it distorts practical enquiries' task. That task is not to sustain social consensus indefinitely, but to distill enduring ideals from the transitory traditions that hatch them. Practical rationalities' main function is not first to perpetuate our inheritances, but to nourish those living traditions from which practical progress springs.

6

Perspectivism and the Limits of Practical Enquiry

The enduring import of the "world loyalty," the fidelity to our practical experience and to our practical inheritances that Whitehead proposes may be not that it strengthens religious conviction but that it attenuates human self-importance and with it the presumption that the ends human agency serves are exclusively human ends. That presumption animates the claim that a rational arché univocally specifies human ends. Yet neither history, nor biology, nor archeology, nor even theology or philosophy has presented convincing evidence that such an arché obtains. The critical mass of evidence contravenes this claim and its operative assumptions: that we confront a singular, morally normative hierarchy of ends, whether specified by God or nature or reason; that our nature is fixed, perhaps even immortal, and in either case underlies the moral norms to which we must conform as conditions of our own good or even salvation; that we have through reason or revelation determinate access to those truths that uniquely identify human ends and the methods conducing to their attainment.

Never have these claims been substantiated as normatively binding, as MacIntyre maintains, on pain of rendering one who rejects them morally or intellectually incontinent. Yet even on Whitehead's account such claims haunt practical enquiry. They do so, however, not as claims to be determinately vindicated, but as operative ideals signaling both that enquiry's enduring faith in reason and its commitment to that faith, to reason's capacity to realize these ideals:

> It is always open to us, having regard to the imperfections of all metaphysical systems, to lose hope at the exact point where

we find ourselves. The preservation of such faith must depend on an ultimate moral intuition into the nature of intellectual action—that it should embody the adventure of hope. (PR:42)

That faith faces continuous challenges flowing from the limits practical rationalities adduce as they incarnate their selective achievements. Yet while those achievements are always subject to criticism, to reconstruction, and to the advance of speculative reason, Whitehead's account suggests a way of sustaining practical enquiries' faith and confidence—optimism, even—while tempering their irrational tendency to mistake their transitory achievements for timeless conditions of rational enquiry's possibility.

Such speculative faith may be preserved first by granting the animating ideal driving Enlightenment theorists' efforts, namely, that moral claims tend toward universalization, without rejecting the entire range of inheritances from which that aim itself took flight. On this count, modern efforts to universalize practical ideals require us neither to reject our inheritances nor to adopt a neutral stance from which to impartially assess competing traditions. Rather, they lead us to acknowledge that many norms specify human ends and goods, all of which might provisionally be resolved by some vision of the good life but none of which will be wholly accounted for in that vision. Such resolutions are endemically selective, embodying valuative patterns constructed from broader possibilities. As such, they lead us also to recognize competing traditions as nonetheless contributing to a shared practical project, and to eschew the insistence that any one tradition's achievements offer a universal, timeless normative arche.

Moreover, practical traditions' achievements ineluctably serve ends beyond their own and are evaluable on those terms as well. Character ideals, for example, would on Whitehead's view be aesthetically as well as morally evaluable. As traditions inhabit an aesthetic teleology, the patterns of conduct they valorize remain subject to aesthetic evaluation. Accordingly, the ends moral traditions thematize and resolve through their exemplary characters, ends abstracted from a broader practical inheritance, are comparable on those terms. Traditions espousing different exemplary characters may then prove mutually evaluable for their aesthetic allure, their capacity to elicit their ideals' reenactment, as well as for their resources' capacity to resolve practical disagreements.

That partial commensurability among traditions does not imply that competing traditions will unilaterally defeat or falsify each other, or even that such an aim is an appropriate task of moral enquiry. Rather, it offers agents the ability to distance themselves from their home traditions sufficiently to engage other traditions' claims without thereby abandoning their commitments, their rationality, their potential for agency. This commensurability thus denies that agents inhabit univocal traditions at all. Instead, it affirms the mass cross-fertilizations traditions bear, the common questions their enquiries face and the common social, economic and political challenges delimiting their practical possibilities. It affirms, moreover, practical enquiry's tendency not to sustain traditions indefinitely but to distill from their local particularities the enduring, enticing ideals for which ages are named.

Fostering those distillations, not securing the univocal supremacy of a single tradition, is practical enquiry's primary aim, as those distillations drive practical progress. As moral enquiry emanates from many traditions, one of its prime tasks will then be to foster substantive, productive engagements among purportedly incommensurable traditions. Such transtraditional exchanges are necessary, even if their ends be barely visible, even if they barely countenance any shared normative standards of discourse and practice, because traditions yield partial truths. Those truths, moreover, unfold as the enquiries they inhabit and the enquiries they face as competitors continually challenge them. That latter point, that practical truths themselves evolve amid their reaffirmations, signals Whitehead's departure from a teleological tradition which seeks to discover eternal, universal moral norms rooted within the cosmos. Yet despite that departure Whitehead honors the operative methodological ideals guiding that tradition, aiming as did its founders to ground his practical enquiries within an adequate cosmological framework:

> A cosmology should above all things be adequate. It should not confine itself to the categoreal notions of one science, and explain away everything which will not fit in. Its business is not to refuse experience but to find the most general interpretive system. . . . Cosmology, since it is the outcome of the highest generality of speculation, is the critic of all speculation inferior to itself in generality. (PR:69)

The enduring insight animating our cosmological "epoch," Whitehead suggests, is that the substance metaphysics upon which Aristotle and his successors founded a particular tradition of practical enquiry embodies a host of premises—the simple location of substances, their

essential endurance, their essential grounding of universal predicates —
now thoroughly discredited by the science to which those premises
helped give rise.[1] The cognate of that point, Whitehead's account suggests, is that the timeless, universal truths such a cosmological order was
alleged to harbor will prove no more eternal than do the substances
alleged to sustain them. They will prove, rather, eternal neither in content nor in form; massively enduring, perhaps, but not timelessly true.

Perspectivism and Practical Truth

The temporalization of truth Whitehead's cosmology implies adumbrates his perspectivism. According to Whitehead, human enquiries
admit two primary fallacies: (1) "simple location," wherein we mistake a
multiply located entity—a quantum particle, for example, for an entity
uniquely located, and (2) "misplaced concreteness," wherein we mistake
a partial for a complete analysis, or a selective set of truths for the whole
range of possible truths from which we abstract that set. These fallacies
riddle a practical tradition that (1) simply locates truth conditions either
in the subjects or in the objects of judgments, rather than in their mutual
inherence, and (2) sees those truth conditions as fixed, rather than as
jointly constituted and jointly evolving. In contrast, Whitehead's account
suggests that practical truth signals an inherently mutable accommoda-
tion between subjects and objects.

Such accommodations afford necessary but never fully determinate
truth conditions. Rather, those conditions are localized both within the
broad teleology and within the actual worlds—the limited perspectives—
their subjects and objects inhabit, and so require contextualization.
Moreover, the normative patterns underlying those contextualizations
include emotional, biological, psychological, and social components,
and only through those components' patternings do agents come to
effect and inhabit rational enquiries. The truth conditions that any
instantiation of rationality supports thus refer to norms or protonorms
themselves evolving and amid which truth criteria may be proposed but
from which they never exclude essential reference.

This contextualization of practical claims' truth conditions illustrates how Whitehead's account both (1) locates practical truth claims
within perspectives, and (2) liberates those claims and the enduring
ideals to which they accord from the perspectives that spawn them.

Thereby his account suggests a perspectivist model of practical enquiry distinct from that MacIntyre excoriates. The perspectivism MacIntyre decries issues from a Nietzschean view asserting that truth claims are localized to perspectives that do not refer to a common world. As such those claims express premises neither potentially univocally binding nor even potentially commensurable, and so permit no rational interchange among their respective adherents:

> (T]he perspectivist challenge puts in question the possibility of making truth claims from within any one tradition. For if there is a multiplicity of rival traditions, each with its own characteristic modes of rational justification internal to it, then that very fact entails that no one tradition can offer those outside it good reasons for excluding the theses of its rivals. (WJ:352)

MacIntyre continues:

> Yet if this is so, no one tradition is entitled to arrogate to itself an exclusive title; no one tradition can deny the legitimacy of its rivals. What seemed to require rival traditions so to exclude and so to deny was belief in the logical incompatibility of the theses asserted and denied within rival traditions, a belief which embodied a recognition that if the theses of one such tradition were true, then some at least of the theses asserted by its rivals were false. (WJ:352)

Yet on MacIntyre's account the logical incompatibility among traditions' theses that he claims perspectivism precludes and practical enquiry presupposes, cannot obtain. For MacIntyre, each tradition sustains a unique set of truth conditions. Yet were that so, traditions' theses would prove neither logically commensurable nor incommensurable. Rather, they would admit no logical relation. To see why we need only recall MacIntyre's insistence that the tenets of logic are insufficient grounds for traditions' engagements. According to MacIntyre, canons of practical rationality require significant contextualization even to identify what claims count as potentially true or false. Yet on that account traditions would face each other not as rational competitors proposing mutually evaluable premises, but as mutually unintelligible rivals.

Moreover, in arrogating viable truth conditions to a single tradition MacIntyre undermines his claim that traditions can rationally defeat their rivals. He argues, for example, that inferior traditions can borrow resources from their superiors and thereby recognize their own short-comings. Yet that process implies an operative rationality functioning within the weaker tradition and conducing to a truth of its own in the process of correcting itself. To that end the theses inhabiting these two traditions would not present themselves as logically incommensurable but as more or less warranted given the evidences and conceptual resources available to both. Indeed, the possibility of traditions compet-ing as rational rivals implies that both have approximated to some shared evidences, some shared truth claims and some mutually recognizable ideals, that is, that their constituent theses are not strictly rationally incommensurable.

According to MacIntyre, perspectivism forestalls the emotivist recourse only by falsely denying practical claims' logical incommensu-rability across traditions. Yet thereby, he maintains, it affirms a view of practical truth inimical to rational enquiry:

> The solution, so the perspectivist argues, is to withdraw the ascription of truth and falsity, at least in the sense in which 'true' and 'false' have been understood so far within the prac-tice of such traditions, both from individual theses and from the bodies of systematic belief of which such theses are con-stitutive parts. Instead of interpreting rival traditions as mutu-ally exclusive and incompatible ways of understanding one and the same world, one and the same subject matter, let us understand them instead as providing very different, comple-mentary perspectives for envisaging the realities about which they speak to us. (WJ:352)

That alleged solution, he maintains, has two problems. First: "the per-spectivist is committed to maintaining that no claim to truth made in the name of any one competing tradition could defeat the claims to truth made in the name of its rivals" (WJ:367). Second:

> The perspectivist, moreover, fails to recognize how integral the conception of truth is to tradition-constituted forms of enquiry. . . . [G]enuinely to adopt the standpoint of a tradition thereby commits one to its view of what is true and false and, in so committing one, prohibits one from adopting any rival standpoint. (WJ:367)

Again, however, MacIntyre's account presupposes a common world to which rival traditions refer as a basis for their rational engagements, while affirming a conception of tradition-constituted rationalities that ensnares their adherents not merely in rival and incompatible traditions, but in rival and incompatible worlds. Each tradition sustains a conception of truth and rationality that cannot in principle lay hold of a common world amid which contested claims might be resolved. For MacIntyre: "The multiplicity of traditions does not afford a multiplicity of perspectives among which one can move, but a multiplicity of antagonistic commitments, between which only conflict, rational or nonrational, is possible" (WJ:367–68). Rational conflict, however, presupposes the ability to move among such positions both as a condition of recognizing traditions as rational rivals, as legitimate alternatives, and of proposing and recognizing resolutions among them.

Such a perspectivist recourse, MacIntyre claims, abandons any commitment to rational enquiry:

> From their [perspectivists'] point of view any conception of truth but the most minimal appears to have been discredited. And from the standpoint afforded by the rationality of tradition-constituted enquiry it is clear that such persons are by their stance excluded from the possession of any concept of truth adequate for systematic rational enquiry. Hence theirs is not so much a conclusion about truth as an exclusion from it and thereby from rational debate. (WJ:368)

Yet again, MacIntyre's account of tradition-constituted enquiries undermines the very possibility of traditions rationally engaging each other. Thereby it undercuts his case against perspectivism, reenforcing the incommensurability he aims to defeat. That consequence results because MacIntyre ascribes both too much and too little normative weight to individual traditions: too much in maintaining that one tradition could be the univocal locus of eternal practical truths; too little in affirming that practical traditions must either prove their rational superiority in toto or contribute little to the progress of practical enquiry.

Conversely, on Whitehead's account practical truths and truth conditions are neither confined to nor wholly independent of particular traditions. Rather, they are multiply located—in traditions, in the inheritances those traditions countenance, and in the partially shared teleology those traditions jointly construct. Practical truths are multiply located, issuing from selections subject to particular truth conditions at particular times, but according to enduring ideals localized in multiple traditions. Such selections render practical truths not univocal but polyvocal, attaching agents' partially shared decisions and judgments to partially shared enduring ideals. Such accommodations realize practical truths always localized but never univocally localized, truths that render their constituent traditions partially commensurable as they arise from and foster a partially shared practical endeavor.

Perspectivism and Practical Progress

The possibility of that shared practical endeavor, Whitehead's account suggests, derives from practical enquiries' ability to criticize and propose enduring ideals and thereby to permit past and present valuations to adumbrate without determining future achievements. That ability enjoins enquirers to ascribe appropriate normative weight both to past achievements and to their future prospects. To that end it implies a perspectivism wherein practical truths are multiply located and evolve over time, as a condition of traditions' making their ideals constructive of the future. Against MacIntyre's charges that perspectivism permits neither practical truths nor practical progress, a Whiteheadian perspectivism permits a progressive account of moral enquiry within which (1) practical ideals accrue truth as they expand the range of valuative potentials their adherents enjoy, and (2) traditions embody truths inhabiting a broader practical enterprise and referant to an aesthetic teleology none can wholly encapsulate.

Traditions' claims and ideals secure truth, accord to that teleology's normative mandates, as they expand the valuative potential, the allure, of the ideals they inherit, recreate, and propose. Practical truths once realized issue from the fleeting actualities that initially instantiate these ideals as their bids for objective immortality. These ideals progress as they adduce novel valuations from subsequent adherents. Their truth value enlarges as they afford living possibilities for subsequent enquirers, expanding their successors' potential for novel enjoyments. Their truth value diminishes as they militate against such prospects. These ideals' truth values are thus subject to the temporal passage of their original instantiations. As the actual worlds effecting those instantiations recede, these ideals must offer more widely appealing possibilities for their recreation, thereby tending toward universalization through the nonlocal recreations they evoke.

At the same time, their histories suggest that such ideals, however universalized, bear joint witness to their enduring import and to their originary instantiations. These ideals do not offer a basis for eternally true or universal practical judgments. Rather, they comprise trans-traditional ideals embodying complex, polyvalent truth values. Their truths endure, but not eternally. Their truths span multiple traditions, yet never shed their local particularities. Rather, these truths recreate the originary conditions and valuations instantiating them, proposing potentially shared enjoyments among traditions. Shared enjoyments construct the patternings of ideals through which traditions distill ideals from their partially shared practical inheritances. Thereby enduring ideals and the traditions hatching them recreate each other, reformulating and thereby enlarging the limited perspectives that spawn novel enquiries and novel ideals.

Conversely, practical ideals surrender truth value when they fail to offer or when they negate live prospects for novel, increasingly complex valuations. As such ideals fail to elicit wide appeal, their efficacy beyond their home perspectives diminishes. Moreover, as the traditions bearing such ideals fail to admit the novel content that might render them more complex and globally instantiable, more inviting, they undercut the ability of their operative truth conditions to admit evidences and ideals beyond their local perspectives. In undermining the potential for shared truth conditions and practical resources among traditions, such perspectives' constituent ideals become less globally efficacious, less constructive beyond their limited instantiations. As they surrender that constructive capacity, such traditions do not merely stagnate, they devolve, their truth conditions unraveling as they become less globally binding.

Amid this contrast between devolution and evolution, practical traditions progress as their ideals conduce to those shared enjoyments through which enquirers enjoy novel values, and to those conditions for engagement whereby enquirers can criticize and recreate such ideals. Exemplifying such progress is the ideal of human perfectability that animates our tradition of practical enquiry as MacIntyre depicts it. Contrary to MacIntyre's account, however, that ideal evolves as the tradition itself evolves. For Aristotle, for example, that ideal embodies a normative cosmology setting forth the principles by which human agents actualize their natural telos. For Aquinas, that ideal is revivified within a theistic cosmology referring the human telos to a divine community. For Kant, that ideal is specified neither by nature nor by God but by reason's constructing within nature a normative teleology enjoining agents to make themselves better than nature made them—to perfect themselves—as a condition of realizing that Kingdom of Ends within which human nature finds its completion.

The broad continuity of that ideals' instantiations can be challenged, as MacIntyre's genealogy suggests, insofar as Kant's account depicts human ends as chosen as well as given by reason, and the moral community underwriting those choices as constructed by agents rather than as specified by norms wholly independent of them. Those ends, however, circumscribe a teleology aiming to perfect such agents. Kant expands the parameters of agency amid which perfectability is pursued, extending such possibilities to all rational agents and positing a range of ends agents may actualize in perfecting themselves. Nevertheless, for Kant as for his premodern predecessors, human ends and choices are delimited by a determinate teleology, a conception of agency, and a vision of moral community all oriented toward human perfectability.

Indeed, on a Whiteheadian account that enduring ideal permits Kant to propose the novel ideal—autonomy—requisite to fostering such a moral endeavor amid his other inheritances. Like Aristotle, Kant unfolds his accounts of practical reason and of moral community amid a normative teleology. To the extent that Kant challenges Aristotle's own perfectionistic project, positing as Aristotle does not autonomous choice among ends, he does so not on moral but on scientific grounds. Kant inherited an understanding of a deterministic universe seemingly inhospitable to human freedom. That inheritance lent him to posit a constructive agency rendering humans agents not by nature but through their construction of an autonomous sphere within nature. Kant's project unravels the Aristotelean arche not because Kant rejects a teleological understanding of the moral enterprise, but because for him as for Aristotle that teleology had to accommodate the claims of science upon the provenance of practical reason.

That teleology, for Kant as for Aristotle, had to afford an adequate accounting of human nature as situated within a broader cosmos. To this end, Kant like Aristotle recognizes that moral enquiry is not isolated from scientific enquiry, that its ideals inhabit a teleology whose adequacy bears substantive practical import. At the same time, while this commitment to teleological adequacy leads him to posit the ideal of autonomy as constitutive of the moral enterprise, it simultaneously undoes his own project, as the scientific understanding he inherited overstated determinism in nature and so overstated the extent to which human agency had to be liberated from that nature. Yet Kant's project founders as does Aristotle's, not because he rejects teleology but because he espouses an inadequate, or better, an incomplete teleology.

While Aristotle and Kant advance incomplete teleologies, however, both set forth enduring exemplars of practical reasoning oriented toward human perfectability. Moreover, in valorizing respectively the natural givenness and the construction of human ends, their projects differentially shade their shared ideals, broadening agents' practical possibilities. Kant's account, for example, emphasizing rational selection among ends, expands the range of options by which we may reconstruct the ideals we inherit. Those enlarged prospects are exemplified by contemporary efforts to conjoin our deontic and virtue inheritances, to reconceive appropriate relations between the right and the good. That inheritance, depicting ends both as created and as given, itself inhabits an enquiry wherein science and technology propose novel visions of perfectability. Indeed, as human nature has proven increasingly reconstructible, the question of what delimits the human telos has itself evolved.

Practical Rationalities and the Aesthetic Teleology

On a Whiteheadian view, the relation between what's given to a human telos and what's constructed through its pursuit cannot help but evolve. To that extent practical enquiries cannot be charged with restricting that evolution, as such restrictions would contravene the former's ends. Rather, such enquiries are charged with approximating to the mandates of an aesthetic teleology, are charged not merely with inducing practical resolutions among perspectives, but with inducing resolutions that afford novel valuative potential. Practical rationalities prove faithful to their task when they aim not to secure definitive resolutions among traditions, but to distill the distinct ideals animating those traditions, and to induce engagements through which traditions' interactions tend toward those distillations, whether in concert or in opposition.

That task is endless, yet admits practical progress as traditions (1) expand the available range of valuative potentials, of living ideals, (2) expand the range of intense, novel valuations possible, and (3) expand agents' capacities to afford such valuations. To that end practical enquiries, in recreating their inheritances, sustain the potential for productive engagements among traditions. Such engagements imply that specific practical enquiries are neither univocally truthful, nor oriented toward one determinate telos. Practical enquiries exhibit no such character, a Whiteheadian account would suggest, because the horizon of inheritance and creativity that they span comprises a triadic vector. Traditions inherit and recreate obdurate rationalities whose mutable practical truths delimit how they transmute their inheritances into future facts. Only as thus recreated will such inheritances become efficacious for the future, yet their novel efficacies will never be again as they once were.

These ineluctably incomplete recreations lay the groundwork for a partially shared inheritance among traditions, and with it the potential for a jointly constructed future. As the ideals traditions yield secure broader valuative capacity, elicit from wider loci vivid valuations, they root themselves wider and deeper within practical enquiries' provenance. At the same time they set forth a range of partially shared ideals about which traditions can dispute in distilling their particular achievements. Those enticing ideals underlie practical engagements through which traditions become at once more integrated (envisaging shared ideals) and more differentiated (differentially countenancing those ideals). Thereby those traditions become more complexly patterned and interrelated, their exchanges guiding the partially shared practical project they jointly inhabit and jointly construct anew.

The enduring ideals differentiating such traditions conduce to their productive engagements when they increase the ability of traditions' adherents to see common inheritances and common possibilities. Those potential recognitions suggest that the truth conditions sustaining these ideals are partial and mutable, localized and nonlocalized, and subject to a broader teleology and a broader practical project to which their productions bear mutual witness. Such engagements attach partly shared ideals and inheritances to partly shared practical problems and prospects, constructing partly shared truth conditions. Thereby, the operative ideals structuring the conceptual distances among traditions permit their adherents to recognize shared practical prospects both in a broader inheritance and in a potentially shared future.

Amid the aesthetic teleology Whitehead depicts, however, such engagements will tend not toward definitively resolving traditions, but toward continually integrating and differentiating them. Indeed, such traditions would not converge even qua ideal. They would tend neither alone nor together toward practical truth per se, but toward a teleology enjoining not practical resolution but the production of novelty. That creative emphasis, however, should neither understate the importance Whitehead assigns to our practical inheritances, nor overstate the tenuous and flickering advance of practical enquiries. Despite his emphasis upon "the creative advance of the universe," Whitehead shares with MacIntyre a reverence for his inheritances. He would maintain—rightly—that to surrender that reverence is to abandon an accurate historical sense, as do alike those scientists who dismiss teleology and those philosophers who disdain scientists—both of whom misapprehend their inheritances.

At the same time, our inheritances embody and are embodied within a normative teleology specifying appropriate relations among past, present, and future, a teleology whose normativity is both recapitulative and creative. To that end, practical enquiries suitably tend their inheritances only when they nourish the latter's constructive possibilities. Conversely, they abandon their task if they commend past achievements' hegemony. To render practical enquiry primarily recapitulative would falsify both its proper task and its proper products, contravening not merely the order of truth but the ethical order Whitehead's teleology embodies. It would contravene that order because the debts we owe to our predecessors obligate us not only to those predecessors but also to our successors. We discharge those debts, Whitehead's account suggests, not by repeating our predecessors' achievements, by constructing well-formed traditions as tributes to a past but dimly uncovered. Rather, we do so by recreating and handing over to our successors a stock of living ideals, ideals not well-formed, not conceptually exhausted, but teeming with possibility.

7

Practical Enquiries

The preceding chapter's conclusions, that practical enquiry comprises multiple styles of reasoning approximating to moral truths and ideals both given and created and revealing a teleology both historical and futural, would signal to MacIntyre the decisive failure of a Whiteheadian account of practical rationality. This account would locate practical enquiry irremediably within the emotivist culture MacIntyre rejects, negating its ability to authoritatively unite moral conviction and rational justification. Moreover, such a position precludes univocal commitment to a single tradition or to a fully determinate hierarchy of human ends and goods. Thereby, it would afford agents no rational standards for their deliberations, but would instead foster interminable practical disputes.

The objection that a perspectivist account of practical rationality cannot unite conviction and justification voices MacIntyre's cognitivist assumption that effecting such a union is rational enquiry's essential function. On a Whiteheadian account, however, that function would be subordinate to the requirement that agents abstract from their own traditions sufficiently to rationally engage other traditions—as a condition of exercising the intellectual virtues Whitehead's account suggests. Among those virtues he would include the traditional wisdom, justice, and courage. Yet he would enjoin also commitments to the ideals of Truth, Beauty, Art, Adventure, and Peace, to universality of judgment, and to adventurous speculation in the service of producing civilizing, enduring ideals.

While practical enquiries thereby encompass conceptual syntheses both recapitulative and creative, their trajectory is futural. The main task of practical ideals is to solicit their future realizations. Accordingly, practical enquiry's primary tasks will be to criticize and to reconstruct the antecedent achievements embodying those ideals: "Each new epoch enters upon its career by waging unrelenting war upon the aesthetic goods of its immediate predecessor" (PR:340). In criticizing prior achievements its aim is not destructive but creative, effecting reconstructed ideals and revivified traditions that replicate the best of their inheritances. Its aim is not to create novelty for the sake of novelty, but novelty for the sake of expanding the valuative possibilities traditions can realize and the satisfactions they can yield.

To these ends practical enquiry's main task cannot be to seamlessly wed moral conviction to rational justification within a single tradition. Such an ideal would be untenable because every tradition bears the limits and contingencies of its origins. Traditions' selective emphases distill their enduring ideals at the cost of rendering themselves irremediably transient. The task of practical rationality, then, is not only to fuse conviction and justification in the service of one ideal but to expand thereby our practical inheritances, and so practical reason's constructive potential, its capacity to effect novel normative syntheses. Moreover, no tradition's convergence upon a univocal hierarchy of goods could prove ever more than provisional, ever more than asypmtotic, ever more than one possibility of integrating those goods.

For those reasons, MacIntyre would deny that traditions thus conceived could evince intelligible, authoritative bases for rational practical judgments. That denial would issue from his claim that the determinate fusion of truth, tradition, and teleology alone affords a viable moral tradition, a tradition able to rationally resolve the substantive moral disagreements arising within it. Yet two untenable assumptions underwrite MacIntyre's claims. First, they assume that rational conflict entails the possibility of enduring rational resolution. That entailment is dubious because, as MacIntyre describes conflicts within ordered traditions, the conditions practical claims must meet to be regarded as rational, much less as true, themselves evolve as practical conflicts proceed. Accordingly, it's unclear how even within a single tradition substantive agreement could be maintained indefinitely. Second, such agreements are unsustainable because traditions' canons of rationality evolve not primarily through rational criticism but through social, political, and economic changes, through conquests and even through osmosis.

Practical enquiries rational evolutions do not embody intellectual histories isolable from their contingent social undercurrents. Traditions' achievements are partial, shifting, and subject to defeat not only by reason but equally by war, by plagues, by conquerors, by bad timing, even by bad weather. The rationalities traditions carve out amid these empirical cross-currents will either fail to exemplify the hermetic arché MacIntyre describes, or will do so by isolating themselves from other traditions such that rational intercourse among them cannot obtain. To tell an intelligible narrative of practical enquiry's history on the scope MacIntyre envisions, then, would on a Whiteheadian account forbid telling a history of rational conflict among well-arrayed traditions. Instead it would require the narrator to depict conflicts among traditions that variously embody the ideals dividing them; conflicts occasionally punctuated by attacks of reason rather than driven by rational engagement; conflicts whose competing ideals were advanced or defeated by forces distinct from their intellectual merit.

A Whiteheadian genealogy, then, would reject MacIntyre's suggestion that intellectual history drives practical ideals' unfolding, an emphasis undercutting MacIntyre's recognition of how socially situated ideals are. This discordance arises because MacIntyre assumes both that ideals are wholly localized within traditions, and that those ideals offer intelligible conceptual resources to rival traditions, such that rational engagement propels traditions' interactions. Conversely, a Whiteheadian genealogy would not depict conflicts among ideals as occuring among the scholars who write up these ideals' life histories. Rather, it would locate those conflicts among the social groups embodying these ideals, ideals advanced or defeated as they secure intelligibility, motive force, and justification among their adherents.

On this account, moreover, practical conflict does not aim only to secure provisional consensus among the adherents of distinct ideals. It aims also to segregate living ideals, those that secure zealous adherents and effect their temporary ascendancy, from inert ideals whose appeal or effectiveness, whose intelligibility and motive force and hence whose potential for rational justification—whose potential truth—has waned. For Whitehead, the truth of a practical ideal does not refer solely to its coherence or consistency with our inheritances or with the competing practical resources other traditions might offer. Rather, that truth also refers essentially to the emotional appeal that incites agents to action in that ideal's development and defense. Only thereby do ideals animate moral projects creative of the future, and only as they underwrite those constructive activities may we deem practical ideals rational in the fullest sense.

A Whiteheadian account of practical rationality thus presents a very different view of the contemporary moral climate than does MacIntyre's. For MacIntyre, maintaining that agents' variously reconstruct moral traditions on the basis of multifaceted ideals and truths emotively vindicated would signal the triumph of emotivism and the demise of practical enquiry. On a Whiteheadian account, in contrast, the emotivist challenge MacIntyre describes would not issue from contemporary agents' inability to premise their claims' intelligibility, motive force, and justification upon a univocal rational standard. Rather it would issue from the assumption that enquirers must secure complete and wholly determinate rational consensus upon appropriate humans ends as a condition of moral agency.

The latter assumption, however, was rejected even by Aristotle, who insisted that we not seek more determinacy in our enquiries than their evidences support. That Aristotle's account retained this indeterminacy proved both a strength and a weakness: a strength in permitting developments of his account's central notions, such as justice, a weakness in that those developments undermined the univocal arche he proposed. Yet such unravelings are inevitable, as these traditions' operative ideals arrange contingencies they can neither wholly rationalize nor permanently hierarchize. Such traditions are never founded de novo, but emerge from the embers of antecedent traditions. Moreover, they are never founded upon a consistent set of eternally true first principles, nor are they isolable from conceptual cross-fertilization. More importantly, no tradition unfurls a unilaterally normative arche of practical ideals and truths. Rather, traditions enact the practices and virtues through which their distinctive norms acquire authoritative content.

The Virtues of Traditions

For these reasons, to expect that any tradition's arche will prove univocally motivating, intelligible, and justified evinces an irrational faith in reason worthy not of Aristotle but of the Enlightenment theorists MacIntyre derides in Aristotle's defense. Indeed, he shares crucial assumptions with his modern rivals. Like them, MacIntyre overemphasizes reason's role in guiding action and delimiting the terms of the good life. Thereby he specifies criteria for practical rationality and human agency that no tradition could satisfy. Enlightenment theorists' failure to univocally specify a determinate set of moral principles may well have shown, as MacIntyre maintains, that practical reason per se does not afford universal normative principles available to all agents. Equally true, however, is that human agency cannot be rendered wholly intelligible within a single tradition. Traditions, rather, espouse ideals and truths whose provisional resolutions are never more than partially realized and partially justified.

This overemphasis upon reason's role in securing and advancing practical principles, moreover, issues from MacIntyre's rejection, again shared with his modern rivals, of a commitment to metaphysical adequacy. MacIntyre argues against Nietzsche and Foucault, for example, that apart from certain metaphysical presuppositions affirming their authorship, their genealogies are unintelligible. Yet MacIntyre's genealogy evinces the same problem. On his insular view of traditions, for example, the Thomist tradition to which he claims allegiance should appear as alien and irrational to him. Yet he does not represent his allegiance as an arational conversion, despite his previous immersion in an emotivist culture whose denizens on his view cannot exercise rational agency.

Moreover, he does not present his transition from an Aristotelean to a Thomist position as such a conversion despite the deep discontinuities between them. Rather, he claims that the latter is superior to the former because the Thomist synthesis includes the insights of both Augustine and Aristotle. Aquinas' synthesis, however, fuses distinct traditions that on MacIntyre's view should have appeared incommensurable. More importantly, Aquinas could not have effected that synthesis were he localized solely in either tradition. Indeed, on MacIntyre's account Aquinas' allegiances refer determinately neither to the traditions he inherited nor to the tradition he constructed, leaving him bereft of rational recourse.

To the extent that Aquinas was able to reconcile his inheritances, however, as was Aristotle before him and Kant after him, his methodological principles were perspectivist, seeking to preserve the best elements among his inheritances. That approach, far from arising recently as the bastard by-product of a misguided modern project, is a transhistorically evident tendency of philosophical enquiry, moral and metaphysical. Such enquiries' progress has been underwritten by those who upheld systematic inclusiveness as a condition of their success. Indeed, even MacIntyre holds out a like inclusiveness as a benchmark whereby traditions prove their adequacy, despite his paradoxical effort to exclude the bulk of such enquiry from rational debate.

That MacIntyre seeks such exclusion is evident in his positing of insular traditions falsely isolated from their heterogeneous inheritances and falsely rendered commensurable only to the extent that one tradition rationally defeats all others. At the same time, MacIntyre grants that tradition itself is a modern idea. Yet he does not admit also that his account of the historical discontinuity among traditions renders his own methodology unintelligible, presupposing as it does the conceptual resources modern enquiries have made available. His bifurcation of modern and premodern traditions could hardly be recognized as accurate by those moderns who conceived their tasks by reference to their inheritances. Moreover, as in their work they too encountered distinct traditions, modern theorists' synthetic, constructive endeavors presuppose a methodological orientation that, like Aquinas', preserved these traditions' insights.

These methodological points illustrate how MacIntyre's own account is hostile to the traditions he aims to defend and alien to the broader tradition of practical enquiry wherein it finds its roots. According to MacIntyre, for example, the Thomist tradition finds inhospitable a culture saturated with negative rights, rights claimed in the service not of a common good but of individuals' autonomy. Yet in opposing that culture, MacIntyre deploys an account of negative traditions, a conceptual artifact requiring that rival traditions be vindicated or vanquished, accorded wholesale rational hegemony or consigned to the scrapheap. On this view traditions cannot contribute resources to each other, cannot mutually develop common themes, cannot acknowledge their common sources, their common questions, their common challenges.

Such a view, far from locating the Aristotelean and Thomist traditions intelligibly within the broader tradition of moral enquiry we've inherited, renders them hegemonic such that they a priori exclude rival traditions from the arena of rational debate. This account renders the enduring ideals and truths limning that broader tradition not live options, but unintelligible artifacts of failed practical projects. It leaves inexplicable why Aristotle's arche failed to survive in toto and why Aquinas' synthesis lost its stranglehold upon medieval Europe. Similarly, it leaves unintelligible how Kant's ideals secured their allegiances and founded their distinctive moral order. Moreover, it renders modern and premodern traditions and their methods mutually incoherent, directed as they often are by distinct inheritances serving disparate ends.

MacIntyre's insular view of traditions not only leaves moral enquiry's broader historical sweep unintelligible, but stands as a bulwark against that enquiry's progress. Indeed, his view reenforces the relativism he despises, particularly insofar as he is not committed to an ideal of metaphysical adequacy. This lack is evident methodologically in his use of narrative genealogy to recount practical enquiry's history. The narrative model of relating historical processes is older than the genealogical method, and so is immune to the criticism that it is a modern invention. Yet this model has the unfortunate tendency to extrude its form upon the content of its study, as a good narrative requires conflict, conflict definitively resolvable.

The tradition MacIntyre assays offers the former, but in a way that does not admit of definitive resolvability. Moral enquiry did not end with Aquinas; it has since afforded other viable syntheses and other grave conflicts and shows no tendency toward enduring resolution. To claim otherwise is to systematically falsify practical enquiry's history and its enduring issue: interminable debate. It is to assert despite massive evidence to the contrary that that history is rational, while rendering it unintelligible. It is to assert that intellectual history drives rather than attends natural and social history. It is to assert reason's independence of these anthropological roots, rendering unintelligible its subjection to their contingencies. It is to claim for intellectual history a normativity it does not evince and to arrogate more truth to a genealogical analysis than, on MacIntyre's own account, such an analysis could offer.

Moreover, in granting intellectual history that status, MacIntyre aims to secure traditions' normativity such that they can rightfully exclude objections, internal or external, that might undermine their rational authority. Yet that view signifies his account's failure to exemplify its own standards of rational enquiry, and its dismissal not only of the traditions he aims to reject but of the traditions he aims to defend. This move undercuts the Aristotelean and Thomist traditions by militating against their methodological premises and the syntheses they effected, which sought to supply universal, systematic accountings of their contemporary philosophical contexts. It repudiates the modern traditions he refuses by failing to absorb those modern conceptual resources his account requires to effectively contest its contemporary rivals.

MacIntyre's account, for example, undercuts genealogy as a viable investigative method. Defending this method would undermine his claims for the isolability and incommensurability of traditions, as he would then adopt alien elements to fortify his own tradition's resources. Conversely, integrating these elements would force him to acknowledge that he cannot defend the tradition he avers by recourse to its own resources alone; that tradition would then fail his own test of conceptual adequacy. Accordingly, while MacIntyre charges against modern theorists that their positions are lacking because they preclude recourse to traditional concepts and methods, this charge is with equal accuracy leveled against his account, which precludes recourse to modern concepts and methods. Indeed, insofar as he employs the methods his inheritance makes available while simultaneously denying their legitimacy, MacIntyre himself uses a technique he criticizes modern theorists for employing.

Moral Truths and Moral Progress

That last difficulty exemplifies the challenge MacIntyre's account of traditions presents to contemporary ethicists, as that account fosters a moral tribalism incompatible with practical enquiry and holding out little hope for its progress. It evinces a hostility toward our inheritances that supersedes the hostility MacIntyre believes Enlightenment theorists show toward their predecessors, or the genealogists toward theirs. In the process this view renders his restorative project self-defeating. It does so by valorizing the least defensible elements of the tradition he defends—the recourse to divine revelation and to tradition per se as objects of proof and to the exclusion of contrary evidence—and by perversely affirming these elements as grounds of intellectual virtue. Thereby his project passes over from moral enquiry into apologetics, dragging with it those elements of the Aristotelian and Thomist traditions that might well remain viable.

In the process he deprives those traditions' enduring ideals not only of a worthy defense, but of the potential legitimacy whereby they might find a home within contemporary moral debate. For MacIntyre, the practical dilemma we confront is plain: revive the ideals he proposes and their requisite practices and virtues in toto, or reject them and surrender to irrationality. That stark choice, however, represents both a false dichotomy and a refusal to practice practical enquiry as he claims we should practice it. It proposes a false dichotomy in that it refuses to grant to these ideals their potential as constructive material for syntheses beyond their original contexts. It undercuts the practice of moral enquiry by assuming standards of truth and progress inimical to each as evidenced by MacIntyre's own genealogy.

On the relation between moral truths and moral progress, MacIntyre and Whitehead are most plainly at odds, and their differences are instructive. According to MacIntyre, moral truth and progress toward that truth obtain only within single traditions. Yet his presentation of Aquinas and Aristotle as exemplars of practical enquiry's progress undermines that claim. Indeed he misrepresents Aristotle and Aquinas on these points, as neither would have recognized himself as operating within an insular tradition, and as both sought to advance practical claims both morally binding and metaphysically adequate. To those ends neither could have maintained that practical truth resided univocally within one tradition, the view of truth MacIntyre claims is a necessary condition of practical enquiry. Rather they would have to reject such a conception as a precondition of their own synthetic methodologies.

Conversely, MacIntyre's tribalism rejects these traditions' aspirations and operative methods, dissolving the conditions under which their ideals might prove intelligible and persuasive to contemporary audiences. Those conditions, underwritten by agents' partially shared inheritances, partially shared practical challenges and partially shared options, permit substantive debate among the contemporary adherents of these ideals. They underlie, for example, contemporary theorists' efforts to develop the virtue component of Kant's practical philosophy. MacIntyre's account, in contrast, insisting to the point of absurdity that Aristotle and Aquinas advance ideals alien to present theorists, despite those ideals' evident influence upon contemporary debates, denies them their role as enduring possibilities. Thereby, his account renders those traditions at best marginal contributors to contemporary debate and at worst a degeneration or blight from which practical enquiry was fortunate to have recovered itself.

On a Whiteheadian account that fate could never befall them. Rather, well-ordered traditions would admit substantive revision through which they would contribute novel ideals and truths to be themselves reconstructed amid their adherents' broader practical inheritances. On this view, moral traditions would develop analogously to how Whitehead conceives the unfolding of individual occasions of experience. Each occasion inherits resources from its past, reconceives those inheritances given its present potential satisfactions, and renders its decision upon that conjunction. Thereby it passes over into objective immortality, its consummation signifying not its wholesale endurance as living satisfaction but its potential for revivification in future satisfactions.

Similarly, enduring traditions inherit practical ideals and truths from their predecessors, countenance them amid the other ideals and truths with which those inheritances compete and effect the decisions signifying their satisfactions. Each set of ideals and truths thus instantiated, each tradition thus realized, has a shelf life. That does not mean that its animating ideals cannot be reenacted, but that they can never again be incarnated as they originally were. Those ideals are thus not rendered irrelevant as their time has passed. Rather to the extent that they remain potential valuative objects, those ideals are both representative of the past and creative of the future, limning those partially shared inheritances amid which distinctive traditions unfold.

Still, each tradition not only marks a decision upon an antecedent state, but embodies a past we can neither revivify nor turn to for univocal authoritative reference. While perpetuating their social embodiments, traditions work primarily to distill the novel ideals that stoke their successors' creativity. To this extent unilateral reference to tradition as the authoritative source of moral ideals thwarts practical progress, denying ideals their creative potential. Indeed, Whitehead suggests that such recourse is not merely contrary to reason but immoral—in two senses. First, univocally reaffirming ideals once functional but presently "out of season" illicitly contravenes those ideals struggling to be born. Second, such references eschew the virtues practical enquiry appropriately conducted cultivates, among them the commitment to intellectual adventure and to a rationalistic optimism representing the future neither as foreclosed nor as imperiled but as a realm of constructive possibility.

A Whiteheadian account of practical rationality, then, would deem MacIntyre's restorative project not merely misguided or rationally deficient but immoral insofar as it wages war with and upon the future. Practical enquiry's primary task, a Whiteheadian account suggests, is not to reconstruct the past but to create the futures that that past envisions. These replicative and creative tasks comprise practical rationality's countervailing tendencies, tendencies it circumscribes only raggedly within traditions, spheres of moral normativity embracing particular truths and ideals. Practical enquiries thus secure for their operative truths and ideals not eternal, universal validity, but tenuous assent among their adherents. These ideals and truths endure insofar as they prove intelligible, motivating, and justified to successive enquirers, and wane insofar as they fail to elicit such enthusiasms. Yet on this account practical rationalities must be recreated if moral enquiries are to discharge their central task, producing those constructive ideals and truths that elicit intense, novel valuations.

Their potential to evoke such responses expands as practical enquiries unfurl their distinctive teleologies and archai. Yet no tradition effects a univocal teleology, a singular authoritative arche, or even a determinative relation between a given teleology and that teleology's espoused ends. Practical progress issues not from securing a singular arche, but from nourishing those interchanges among traditions that expand our practical possibilities. The truth test of the ideals and practical claims thus proposed is not their univocity but their potential intelligibility, motive force, and justification to successive adherents. Conversely, practical rationalities tend toward greater inclusiveness as they aim to challenge and reconstruct their inheritances. To that end, practical enquiry's primary task is not to unite conviction and justification in the service of a narrow range of ideals, and thereby to resolve practical conflict by precluding it. Rather, its main aim is to foster conditions under which agents can productively pursue moral conflict, and so to maximize their range of practical prospects.

This aim, moreover, does not imply that practical conflicts must be resolvable to be productive. Quite the contrary: it suggests that some practical conflicts must remain unresolved as a condition of moral progress. Such conflicts include those among virtue, deontic, and utilitarian theorists, whose competing ideals do not undercut but evoke the construction of a partially shared practical inheritance. This inheritance conditions these traditions of practical enquiry, however they effect their departures from it. Such traditions, then, may be seen to advance resources from which contemporary agents might reconstruct their practical possibilities. In thus appropriating their inheritances, of course, agents inevitably reanimate the formers' questions, incoherencies, and potential conflicts with their competitors. Yet practical enquiries' primary task here is not to secure wholesale resolutions but to build novel syntheses from their inheritances, syntheses that may prove functional for a time but that ineluctably pass over into their successors.

Amid these transitions, some of each enquiry's incipient rationality, embodied in its operative ideals, truths, and reasoning patterns will endure, while some will be lost. That point acknowledges that, while they may come to function transtraditionally, practical resources also cling to the specificity of their original instantiations, these localizations precluding their enduring in toto. Yet because these constraints obtain, the resources traditions elaborate must not be vanquished but sustained as lasting potentials. They must be cultivated, not despite but in and through their variety, because they present enduring ideals neither self-sufficient nor univocally true but through which we might intelligibly appropriate our inheritances. Indeed, only taken together do these resources make our present inheritance, in its teeming variety, partially intelligible.

Moreover, we must cultivate these resources because they guide the productive practical conflicts that will prove not present but future agents' task to resolve. Reference to the future as a condition for assessing current formulations extends Aristotle's insight that we can evaluate the representatives of practical traditions—be they individuals or ideals—only upon their passing from the historical scene, that is, in terms the present cannot afford. More importantly, it acknowledges that in a battle between the past and the future, the past can never finally emerge victorious. The past endures, but neither in its entirety nor even in the form it originally assumed. By force or by fraud, by rational consent or by default, the future belongs to the future. To deny that point is to reject wholly the optimism that Whitehead maintains animates practical enquiries' progress. It is to affirm that no progress can emerge from current resources. It is to rain upon practical reason a dark age issuing not from the rejection of tradition, but from the impoverishment of a view that has lost faith in its ability to reanimate that tradition. It is to abandon the practical faith that alone conduces to virtue and to truth.

Conclusion

Practical Rationalities

In developing this Whiteheadian account of practical enquiries, I have argued that MacIntyre's own genealogies contravene his central conclusions. Against the insular traditions he posits, I have maintained that practical enquiries originate locally but spawn transtraditional ideals aspiring to universality. Against his claim that rational authority inhabits a singular telos, I have argued that practical rationalities countenance many perfections. Against his insistence that practical rationality requires the wholesale resolution of practical disputes, I have maintained that traditions construct such resolutions provisionally, from an emotive base unfurling amid a processive teleology. Moreover, I have suggested, practical rationalities are as much the products as the producers of such resolutions.

That last point underlines Whitehead's suggestion that practical claims secure truth in several complementary ways: as propositional truths corresponding to our judgments, as perceptual truths corresponding to our experiences, as functional truths corresponding to our experiences' incipient normativities, and as symbolic truths corresponding to the recreations we effect upon our experiences from within the aesthetic teleology harboring them. Practical truths, this account implies, are multifaceted; they signify increasing mutual adaptations between the given elements of our experience and their recreations, and come to admit those creations, those valuations, as factual referents that become themselves givens, and are themselves subject to time, to the demand that they be perpetually reaffirmed. These truth conditions impose themselves upon us, embodying as they do the teleological norms that underwrite our experience.

To this extent, practical traditions must be continually reconstructed, a process underscoring how Whitehead's work adumbrates a partially cognitivist account of practical rationalities issuing from an emotive base. For Whitehead, the truth modes human experience reveals jointly elicit subjects' emotive responses to approximate more massively and intensely both to those experiences' local origins and to their universal, enduring aspirations. Experiences are intense and novel insofar as they are truthful, according themselves to their local inheritances, their present purposes, their future prospects, and the broader teleological ends they serve. Yet such accommodations occur whether those experiences accord to propositional and perceptual or to functional and symbolic data. Past constructions, past valuations, thus become social facts, no less subject to the need for reenactment, yet no less binding upon future reenactments than are perceptual or propositional data.

On this count, values do not signify non-natural facts mysteriously soliciting practical judgments. Rather, facts signify a species of value. For Whitehead, practical truth modes and the facts they designate are subject to our interests, purposes, and inheritances; they signify selected and thus valued experiences. Yet such valuations undercut the rank subjectivism emotivism proposes, as the emotive bases of these selective experiences emanate from shared inheritances, shared purposes, and shared prospects. Moreover, those selections attend truth conditions that evince an elemental normativity, a teleological trajectory orienting them toward a faithful accordance to ends transcending their own.

That fidelity, the "world-loyalty" a Whiteheadian account would ascribe to all enduring valuations, implies that the ends, ideals, and principles thus proposed are subject to truth conditions both inherent in experience and inherently evolving. Any selection's, any tradition's claims submit to truth conditions given in its experience, recreated amid that experience, and passed over as givens for reconstruction. To occur truthfully such claims must accord—perceptually, propositionally, functionally, and symbolically—not only with that tradition's past inheritances and present prospects but also with its future aspirations. Yet to that extent its creations and recreations are neither fictitious nor wholly subjective. Rather, they conform with their inheritances, purposes, and prospects only under the auspices of broader teleological ends.

To these ends, this account suggests, practical enquiry as a practice cultivates and is cultivated by five virtues: Truth, Beauty, Art, Adventure, and Peace. It is truthful in being pluralistic, serving multiple and multiply located ends and purposes; it is beautiful in eliciting and embodying the perfectionistic ideals it envisages; it is adventurous in according its emotive origins with the traditions, practices, and ideals that lend form and discipline to those inchoate origins, minting thereby novel perfections; it is artful in constructing from its local inheritances, purposes, and prospects, ideals that aspire to universality; it is peaceful in securing provisional social consensus, in organizing social life such that practical achievements can be widely and deeply enjoyed, can accrue the intensity and massivity of vivid artistic achievement.

In cultivating these virtues, practical traditions exhibit both their substantive and their processive nature. Their substantive bases take root amid their immediate purposes and challenges, recreating the practices, ideals, and principles they inherit. Yet those recreations occur vis-à-vis other traditions confronting like challenges. These traditions' constitutive truth claims will prove mutually intelligible, motivating, and justified insofar as they are recognized as competitors, as living options. But they will not offer grounds for univocal assent, as they will secure truth only by also serving the ends of novelty and intensity, and will do so only as they evoke novel practical propositions and contrasts among them. This open-endedness renders practical enterprises—irremediably—intellectual adventures. Each tradition aims to propose a mode of practical life securing broad assent, a transcendent, enduring ideal. Yet such ideals inevitably bear their birthmarks. Moreover, the traditions spawning them are not their final arbiters. Rather, these ideals are reaffirmed only as they prove enticing, viable—truthful—to succeeding traditions.

The truths of practical claims and ideals are thus temporally restricted, perpetuated as they evoke both practical assent and lively dispute, dissipated as they fail that task. Their reaffirmation renders such ideals both substantive givens, normative facts, and artistic creations. For Whitehead, practical ideals are aesthetic, deriving their moral import from their ability to elicit distinctive perfections. They are aesthetic in affording satisfactions to appetitive experiences—motives, interests, feelings—that accord most broadly and deeply, hence most truthfully, to his teleology's ends. Such ideals effect coherence among those ends and the experiences of particular subjects. Yet those experiences are conditioned by our shared inheritances, purposes, and prospects. A tradition's animating ideals thus delimit the kinds of satisfactory order and perfection that tradition permits. This pattern of consensual experience, which includes moral experience, exemplifies what Whitehead terms "truthful beauty," creativity in accordance with the self-transcendent mandates his teleology depicts.

In this sense, practical enquiry—perspectival, perfectionistic, emotive, and rational—both discovers and constructs truthful judgments, claims, and mandates. Its perspectivism depicts its substantive and processive nature, its local origins and universal aspirations. Its perfectionism depicts the ends, ideals, and principles it proposes, and the perpetual challenges such proposals confront. Its emotive force signifies its roots in agents' interests, purposes, and prospects, and the transcendent ideals that structure those aims. Its rationality signifies its determinate achievements, the coherent, intelligible, reasoning patterns it builds amid those emotive sources, and the teleological ends it thereby uncovers, and to which it lends voice.

Practical Traditions and Practical Truths

The virtues securing for traditions their rationality—Truth, Beauty, Art, Adventure, and Peace—mandate for those traditions a dual function. Such traditions are essentially creative, reconstructing their received materials into novel patterns. At the same time, those achievements seek to elicit broad assent, consensus—peace. They aim to link the intelligibility and motive force of their animating ideals to a justificatory pattern able to secure social cohesion and so to reproduce itself. This aim at rational resolution seeks depth and massivity, as the broader the coherencies a tradition effects among its inheritances, the greater its practical achievement and its practical potential. Yet to the extent that such resolutions serve a tradition's flourishing, that tradition must admit a plurality of reasoning patterns and operative ideals, a broad base of practical resources from which it might effect and extend such resolutions. Enduring traditions must admit such resources because their past and present achievements, however impressive, embody satisfactions at once enticing and transitory.

Upon distilling its operative ideals, the social coordinations a tradition effects must be recreated, always amid competing ideals and the demand for novel resolutions among them. This process indicates both how practical enquiries can propose true propositions, and how such propositions' incommensurability sustains practical rationalities. For Whitehead, practical propositions approximate to enduring truths. They are selective, limited, and partial, not only because they are constructed, but also because they carry their originary conditions with them. Intense and novel experience requires limitation, as does all aesthetic production. That limitation, though, should remind us both that our achievements are drawn from a broader range of possibilities, and that those achievements that once may have served us well may no longer do so if pressed beyond their practical limits.

We inevitably exceed those limits, Whitehead suggests, when we mistake particular achievements for univocal, timeless truths. Such demands seek to effect consensus where none exists, undermining practical enquiry's prime function. That function is not first to secure social resolutions, but to evoke and sustain the contrasts among ideals that incite practical traditions to propose novel perfections. Practical ideals are not self-perpetuating, nor is their truth static. Rather, their truth claims emanate from the purposes they serve, the prospects they hold out, the aspirations they permit. Conversely, failing to entice potential adherents on those grounds, the intelligibility and motive force, hence the truth potential of those claims, dissipate.

That last point highlights the futural trajectory of practical traditions' achievements. To secure truth, traditions' proposals must not only aim to secure present consensus, but must also solicit their reaffirmation, and so must appeal to a broad base of adherents. To secure broad-based assent, those proposals must solicit the inchoate emotive commitments that incite practical enquiry, and thereby justificatory activities, in the first place. The discovery and recreation of practical propositions is thus first an emotive matter; propositions appear intelligible and workable and purposive before they become candidates for rational justification. The reasoning patterns traditions admit even as potentially justifiable are drawn, then, from the emotive patterns that traditions' originary purposes, interests, and prospects present.

While such reasoning patterns are underwritten emotively before they are rationally appropriated, however, they approximate to distinctive, enduring truths only as they accommodate to broader teleological ends. Whitehead's account, like MacIntyre's, suggests that practical reason embodies a practice requiring faithful cultivation. For Whitehead, however, the originary vision distilling a particular tradition's operative ideals inevitably wanes. To advance, that tradition must render those ideals intelligible and thereby potentially justifiable to new adherents. To do so that tradition must expand the range of discourse and practice it permits, and so confront its rational limits. Those limits, however, are not foremost limits of substantive incommensurability among traditions. They are, rather, limits in any one tradition's capacity to solicit intense emotive response, to seem motivating and potentially intelligible and thus potentially justified to new adherents.

Practical Rationalities and the Emotivist Challenge

The limited capacity of particular traditions to secure social consensus bears emphasis, because it animates the emotivist challenge. In their efforts to combat emotivism, both MacIntyre and his Enlightenment-inspired competitors seek to forestall rational incommensurability across traditions. For MacIntyre, that incommensurability indicates our current conceptual disarray, which we can repair by recurring to a univocal, substantive account of the good life. For his competitors, that incommensurability signals our failure to transcend our localization in a plurality of substantive traditions; uncovering the universal conditions of such traditions would remove their apparent incommensurability, permitting rational social consensus and thereby undercutting the emotivist charge that practical debates admit no practical agreements.

Both approaches, however, seek to justify an account of practical reason prior to identifying the potential motive force or intelligibility of that account's operative ideals. For MacIntyre, practical reason's task is to unify the intelligibility, motivational capacity, and justification of a tradition's operative ideals from within that tradition, effecting the univocal consensus that for him defines practical rationality. Yet his critics argue rightly that this particularist account is circular, defining as rational only those ideals his position embodies. For his competitors, social consensus requires a universal account of practical reason available to and binding upon all rational agents. Yet MacIntyre argues rightly against these universalist efforts that they presuppose an Enlightenment-inspired universalism, an Enlightenment tradition, that they cannot transcend.

Here, as MacIntyre indicates, we are left with a stalemate. Worse still, we are left with the emotivist recourse, denying as it does that practical claims are adjudicable. Yet this stalemate persists only upon the dubious cognitivist assumption that all three views presuppose, namely, that practical enquiry must secure wholesale resolution among competing claims as a condition of its rationality. Such an insistence is itself fairly novel, an artifact of the Enlightenment understanding of universal, procedural reason that both MacIntyre and his emotivist foes rightly reject. Moreover, little in practical enquiry's history commends this view; MacIntyre's own geneaologies speak against it. And while this assumption affirms the universal provenance of practical reason per se, a view MacIntyre aims otherwise to reject, it also embodies a traditional functional psychology that segregates reason from its emotive and appetitive concomitants.

In presupposing that psychology, however, while denying its metaphysical bases, MacIntyre, like his competitors, rejects the teleology traditionally held to link those elements. Thereby, these accounts not only affirm the priority of practical ideals' justification over their motive force, but render unintelligible how practical reason might unify the two. MacIntyre's universalist competitors hold that acknowledging a practical claim's rational justification motivates one to act upon it, lest one fall into a contradiction. Yet they never make clear why inconsistency signals a moral failing, much less why consistency per se is morally mandatory. For MacIntyre, practical enquiry seamlessly links practical ideals' justification and motive force. Yet because they are thus hermetically sealed, the tradition he avows must appear unintelligible to those outside it. Both positions, then, are not merely incommensurable but are in principle rationally unavailable to those who do not a priori share their presuppositions about practical reason's provenance.

On a Whiteheadian account, this result would reflect a misunderstanding of practical enquiry's proper functions and the conditions under which it labors. Practical traditions, I've suggested, inhabit an aesthetic teleology specifying ends to which practical truths at best approximate, and at best transiently. Like MacIntyre's, this account initially locates traditions' animating ideals amid their originary purposes and prospects. Yet those ideals serve ends beyond their originary ends as a condition of their enduring truth. Such ideals, then, not only perpetuate their home traditions, but also reinvigorate the broader teleology those traditions inhabit. Thereby, these ideals expand the range of living ideals and thus of novel satisfactions, of novel achievements—of novel perfections—open to us.

Practical Enquiries and Practical Progress

That progress is the central imperative practical enquiries serve, and to this end their ability to secure social consensus is strictly and rightly limited.

Living traditions advance or regress; they cannot simply endure. To shore up past achievements, as MacIntyre commends, or to establish a foundational procedural basis for establishing enduring practical consensus, as many universalists seek, undercuts practical enquiries' aim. As Whitehead suggests, traditions embody adventures aimed at perfectability. Their achievements, however, are inevitably recreated, and recreated amid perfections beyond their own. Traditions cannot help but countenance these competing perfections, for only as thus perpetually challenged do their own achievements serve the central imperative driving our practical endeavors: the urge not only to live or to live well but to live better.

It is the absence of this injunction, and the metaphysical commitments it embodies, the practical faith, even, that renders the incommensurability of contemporary debates so troubling, and the emotivist challenge so sharp. This absence issues from the rejection, shared by MacIntyre and his contemporary competitors, of a teleological understanding of human experience. Here, even MacIntyre counsels forbearance, lest we embroil ourselves anew in Aristotle's flawed metaphysical biology. On MacIntyre's own criteria however, the more appropriate response to Aristotle's flawed metaphysics would be not to reject it, central as it is to our practical heritage, but to reject only its inadequate elements. That's precisely what Whitehead does, offering a novel teleology rooted in a scientific cosmology consonant with the broadest range of experience available to him.

More importantly, Whitehead's account underscores a point both MacIntyre and his universalist competitors overlook. As already indicated, the belief that practical enquiry must secure wholesale rational consensus as a condition of its rationality seems to me itself irrational. It has no basis even in MacIntyre's genealogies. Yet this irrationality stokes the emotivism both MacIntyre and his competitors rightly resist. Here, irrationality breeds irrationality. It does so not because contemporary theorists fail to offer univocal consensus, but because, in their mania for securing such consensus, in their narrow cognitivism and its fetish for justificatory concerns, they fail to cultivate and to nourish and to revivify the compelling ideals that might secure broad assent. Among such ideals, first and foremost, must stand the conviction that the central aim of practical life is not to secure consensus but to pursue human perfectability in all possible forms.

Historically, ideals of human perfectability have given flight to our practical aspirations; today, the quiescence of such ideals desicates contemporary debate. As Whitehead's account suggests, it is the impoverishment of our vision and imagination, not our conceptual disarray or lack of practical consensus, that imperils the intellectual adventure practical enquiry properly embodies. Indeed, that practical enquiry embodies such an adventure may be the key insight a Whiteheadian account introduces into current proceedings, again, on MacIntyre's terms. As a historical matter, emotivism hardly presents a new challenge. Still, it is now unusually widespread, an artifact, in part, of the moral confusion that MacIntyre so insightfully documents. Most striking about emotivism's contemporary ascent, however, is not its breadth but its shallowness. It owes that ascent, I suggest, not to the conviction it evinces for the pallid view that moral life and practice are matters of preference alone. Rather, it arises from our current resignation, from the belief that, having thus far failed to secure wholesale practical consensus, the traditional impetus toward perfectability must be dispensed with, its demands dismissed as illusory, its metaphysical vestiges rooted out.

Yet as Whitehead's account suggests, only those ideals that evoke aspirations beyond the narrow confines of our individual lives and preferences animate moral convictions properly understood. Such an account makes incarnate the practical faith in human perfectability, the faith in moral progress, that practical enquiry presupposes. Cultivating that faith requires us to cultivate also the intellectual virtues of Truth, Beauty, Art, Adventure, and Peace, those virtues through which we might best revivify our inheritances. It requires us, moreover, not only to recreate our inheritances but to reanimate the aspirations they envision, passing them on to our successors as living options. We must endeavor, then, not only to reap our predecessors' achievements, but to sow our successors' future prospects. Only this orientation to the future permits us to properly appropriate our varied inheritances, to receive them not as irremediably hostile competitors, but instead as practical possibilities admitting of many conjoint realizations. Only such appropriations allow us to properly understand the enduring practical debates we face, to recognize them not as destructive but as constructive, as harbingers not of vice but of virtue.

Notes

1. The Emotivist Challenge

1. Alasdair MacIntyre, *After Virtue: A Study in Moral Theory* (Notre Dame, Ind.: University of Notre Dame Press, 1991). Henceforth AV.

2. Cf. also MacIntyre's "Hume on 'Is' and 'Ought,'" in his *Against the Self-Images of the Age: Essays on Ideology and Philosophy* (Notre Dame, Ind.: University of Notre Dame, 1984).

3. Alasdair MacIntyre, *Whose Justice? Which Rationality?* (Notre Dame, Ind.: University of Notre Dame Press, 1988). Henceforth WJ.

4. Alasdair MacIntyre, *Three Rival Versions of Moral Inquiry: Encyclopaedia, Genealogy, and Tradition* (Notre Dame, Ind.: University of Notre Dame Press, 1990). Henceforth TRV.

5. Alasdair MacIntyre, *First Principles, Final Ends and Contemporary Philosophical Issues* (Milwaukee: Marquette University Press, 1990). Henceforth FP.

2. MacIntyre on Moral Traditions

1. A. J. Roque's "Language Competence and Tradition-Constituted Rationality," *Philosophy and Phenomenological Research*, LI-3 (1991): 611–17, makes a similar point. Commenting on MacIntyre's contention that accepting a rival tradition as rationally superior to one's own requires one to learn a "second first language" (WJ:374–75), Roque argues that: "MacIntyre's questionable appeal to the intuition that an adult can . . . learn a second first language contradicts the claim it is sup-

posed to support, that rationality is tradition-constituted, by postulating a cognitive faculty common to all human beings, . . . [the ability] to acquire a second first language at any stage of their lives" (Roque:617).

2. R. P. George's "Moral Particularism, Thomism, and Traditions," *Review of Metaphysics* 42 (1989): 593–605, makes an analogous point, arguing that if standards of rationality are wholly confined to individual traditions, the conversions MacIntyre describes will be arbitrary: "If, however, such choices are necessarily arbitrary, then there seems to be no way of avoiding a fundamental and decisive relativism in practical reasoning and, therefore, in moral and political theory" (George:598).

3. For a sustained treatment of these themes, cf. Onora O'Neill's "Kant After Virtue," *Inquiry* 26 (1983): 387–406.

4. Immanuel Kant, *Anthropology from a Pragmatic Point of View*, trans. Victor L. Dowdell (Carbondale: Southern Illinois University Press, 1978). Henceforth AN.

5. Immanuel Kant, *Grounding for the Metaphysics of Morals*, trans. in J. W. Ellington's *Immanuel Kant: Ethical Philosophy* (Indianapolis: Hackett, 1983). Henceforth GR.

6. Immanuel Kant, *Metaphysical Principles of Virtue*, trans. in J. W. Ellington's *Immanuel Kant: Ethical Philosophy* (Indianapolis: Hackett, 1983). Henceforth MPV.

7. Cf. Richard McCarty "Kantian Moral Motivation and the Feeling of Respect," *Journal of the History of Philosophy* 31.3 (1993): 421–35, and Larry Hinmann "On the Purity of Our Moral Motives: A Critique of Kant's Account of the Emotions and Acting for the Sake of Duty," *Monist* 66 (1983): 251–67.

8. Cf. Walter E. Schaller, "Kant on Virtue and Moral Worth," *Southern Journal of Philosophy* 25 (1987): 559–73, and Robert B. Louden "Kant's Virtue Ethics," *Philosophy* 61 (1996): 473–89. Louden, in particular, argues that Kant's position fits neatly neither into the deontological nor into the virtue typologies but includes elements of both.

9. For a detailed treatment of Kantian moral deliberation, cf. Barbara Herman, "Obligation and Performance: A Kantian Account of Moral Conflict," in *Identity, Character, and Morality*, ed. O. Flanagan and A. O. Rorty (Cambridge: MIT Press, 1990).

10. Michael Maxwell, in "A Dialectical Encounter between MacIntyre and Longeran on the Thomistic Understanding of Rationality," *International Philosophical Quarterly* 33.4 (1993): 385–99, argues that MacIntyre's defense of Thomism is incoherent in that "MacIntyre

attempts to say something true about all traditions of enquiry while at the same time maintaining that the norms grounding this claim are not trans-traditionally normative" (Maxwell:399). That incoherency derives, Maxwell maintains, from MacIntyre's insistence that the norms of rational enquiry are wholly tradition-constituted, an insistence inconsistent with the tradition he claims to defend: "Thomism has in fact achieved an understanding of rationality that grounds trans-traditional norms of rationality because it makes sense of the rationality of all traditions of enquiry" (Maxwell:399).

11. Robert P. George, in "Moral Particularism, Thomism, and Traditions," *Review of Metaphysics* 42 (1989): 593–605, argues that inherence in such a tradition is not essential insofar as: "No particular self-understanding is required to understand and affirm the set of basic practical principles which, according to Thomists, on the one hand underlie all coherent practical thinking, and on the other distinguish fully reasonable from defective practical judgments. One's grasp of these principles does not depend upon any prior commitment to Thomism" (George:600).

12. According to MacIntyre, well-ordered traditions must be open to such confrontations, hence open to fundamental revisability, as a condition of their truth claims. Thomas Hibbs, however, argues in "MacIntyre, Tradition, and the Christian Philosopher," *Modern Schoolman* (1991): 211–23, that the Thomist tradition MacIntyre purports to defend "is not susceptible of radical revision in the way MacIntyre suggests traditions are" (Hibbs:219). Indeed, he claims, "in what Christianity moves towards—the consummation of all things in Christ—it is at odds with MacIntyre's view of tradition" (Hibbs:219).

13. Peter J. Mehl, "In the Twilight of Modernity: MacIntyre and Mitchell on Moral Traditions and Their Assessment," *Journal of Religious Ethics* 19.1 (1991): 21–54, argues that MacIntyre "tacitly assumes" that agents inhabiting different traditions share some minimal degree of rationality: "Presumably rival traditions share something that somehow enables them to solve some disagreements, because MacIntyre insists that relativism and perspectivism are not the consequences of his understanding of rationality" (Mehl:23, 35).

14. S. Feldman, in "Objectivity, Pluralism, and Relativism: A Critique of MacIntyre's Theory of Value," *Southern Journal of Philosophy* 24 (1986): 307–20, argues that this fluidity signals a substantive difficulty for MacIntyre's claim that agent life-narratives are the subject of moral eval-

uation: "The narrative, or moral biography, of a life is the basis for the moral judgment of that life. Thus, if one life is treated in different ways, then different moral judgments arise about the same person. A trait which is a virtue in one acount is seen as a character flaw in another" (Feldman:313).

15. MacIntyre rejects Aristotle's "metaphysical biology," maintaining instead that tradition-constituted rationality suffices to vindicate a particular virtue tradition: Thomism. Russell Hittinger, however, in "After MacIntyre: Natural Law Theory, Virtue Ethics, and Eudaimonia," *International Philosophical Quarterly* 29 (1989): 449–61, maintains that absent such a 'realist' basis "we are unable to rise to a fully philosophical explication and defense of one or another morality as a concrete way of life" (Hittinger:454).

3. Traditions of Enquiry

1. Cf. chapter 3 in Whitehead's *Science and the Modern World* (New York: Macmillan, 1925). Henceforth SMW.

2. A. N. Whitehead, *The Function of Reason* (Princeton, N.J.: Princeton University Press, 1929). Henceforth FR.

3. A. N. Whitehead, *Process and Reality,* ed. D. R. Griffin and D. W. Sherburne (New York: Macmillan, 1978). Henceforth PR.

4. Cf. also pp. 23–24 in D. W. Sherburne's *A Key to Whitehead's Process and Reality* (New York: Macmillan, 1966), Cf. also the descriptions of eternal objects in chapter 4 (pp. 165–201) of J. L. Nobo's *Whitehead's Metaphysics of Extension and Solidarity* (Albany: State University of New York Press, 1986).

5. Cf. PR:74, 105, 164, 244.

6. Whitehead, quoted in D. W. Sherburne's *A Key to Whitehead's Process and Reality*, p. 31.

7. A. N. Whitehead, *Religion in the Making* (New York: Macmillan, 1926). Henceforth RM.

8. Cf. also Donald L. DuBois' "Reason in Ethics: A Whiteheadian Perspective," unpublished dissertation, University of St. Louis, 1970.

9. A. N. Whitehead, *Adventures of Ideas* (New York: Macmillan, 1933). Henceforth AI.

14. A. N. Whitehead, *The Aims of Education* (New York: Macmillan, 1929). Henceforth AE.

5. Whitehead's Aesthetic Teleology

1. Previous efforts to develop the ethical implications of White-head's metaphysical system include those proposed by Ronald DuBois's "Reason in Ethics: A Whiteheadian Perspective," unpublished dissertation, St. Louis University, 1970, and Lynne Belaief's *Towards a Whiteheadian Ethics* (Lanham, Md.: University Press of America, 1984). Such efforts, however, have been contramanded by arguments such as those proposed by D. L. Schindler in "Whitehead's Inability to Affirm a Universe of Value," *Process Studies* 13 (1983): 117–31, and S. Janusz and Glenn Webster's "The Problem of Persons," *Process Studies* 20.3 (1991): 151–61, which maintain that Whitehead's metaphysics affords neither the normative framework nor the bases for agency required to sustain a viable theory of practical reason.

2. Cf. James Mannoia's "Is God an Exception to Whitehead's Metaphysics?," in *Process Theology*, ed. Ronald H. Nash (Ada, Mich.: Baker Press, 1984), pp. 253–79, and Robert Mesle's "Added on Like Dome and Spire: Wieman's Later Critique of Whitehead," *Process Studies* 20 (1991): 37–53.

3. Cf. Donald A. Crosby's "Whitehead's God and the Dilemma of Pure Possibility," in *God, Values, and Empiricism*, ed. Creighton W. Peden (Macon, Ga.: Mercer University Press, 1989), and Ivor Lecclerc's "The Problem of God in Whitehead's System," *Process Studies* 14 (1985): 301–15.

4. Cf. Robert Neville's *Creativity and God: A Challenge to Process Theology* (Albany: State University of New York Press, 1995), pp. 3–20.

5. For a statement of the former position, cf. Donald W. Sherburne's "Decentering Whitehead," *Process Studies* 15 (1986): 83–94; for a statement of the latter position, cf. John Cobb Jr.'s "A Response to Neville's 'Creativity and God,'" *Process Studies* 10 (1980): 97–105.

6. Cf. Daniel Thero's "Whitehead's God and the Problem of Evil," *Dialogue* 35 (1993): 33–40, and Maurice R. Barineau's "Whitehead and Genuine Evil," *Process Studies* 10 (1990): 181–88.

7. Cf. J. P. Moreland's "An Enduring Self: The Achilles' Heel of Process Philosophy," *Process Studies* 17 (1988): 193–99, and S. Janusz and G. Webster "The Problem of Persons," *Process Studies* 20 (1991): 151–61.

8. For a thorough discussion of these processes, cf. J. L. Nobo's *Whitehead's Metaphysics of Extension and Solidarity* (Albany: State Uni-

versity of New York Press, 1986), chapters 6 and 8, and Ivor LeClerk's *Whitehead's Metaphysics: An Introductory Exposition* (Bloomington: Indiana University Press, 1975), chapters 13 and 14.

9. Cf. George Wolf's "Psychological Physiology from the Standpoint of a Physiological Psychologist," *Process Studies* 11 (1981): 274–91.

10. Cf. P. A. Bogaard's "Whitehead and the Survival of Subordinate Societies," *Process Studies* 21.4 (1992): 219–26.

11. Cf. Lewis Ford's "The Origin of Subjectivity," *Modern Schoolman* 62 (1985): 265–76 and "Subjectivity in the Making," *Process Studies* 21.1 (1990): 1–24.

12. That difficulty, it would seem, stems inevitably from MacIntyre's rejection of the metaphysical bases amid which Aristotle's teleology could function determinately. Indeed, in his subsequent work—*Three Rival Versions of Moral Inquiry*—he proceeds to affirm a Thomist ground for that teleology, a ground implicating a "complex and metaphysical account of the identity and continuity of human beings" (TR:197).

6. Perspectivism and the Limits of Practical Enquiry

1. Cf. Whitehead's account of that complex inheritance in his *Science and the Modern World* (New York: Macmillan, 1925), chapters 3 through 7. Cf. also his account of the rise of that science in his *Adventures of Ideas* (New York: Macmillan, 1933), chapters 8 through 10.

Bibliography

Barineau, Maurice. "Whitehead and Genuine Evil." *Process Studies* 10 (1980): 181–88.

Belaief, L. *Towards a Whiteheadian Ethics*. Lanham: University Press of America, 1984.

Bogaard, P. A. "Whitehead and the Survival of Subordinate Societies." *Process Studies* 21.4 (1992): 219–26.

Cobb, John Jr. "A Response to Neville's 'Creativity and God.'" *Process Studies* 10 (1980): 97–105.

Cobb, John, Jr., and David Ray Griffin. *Process Theology: An Introductory Exposition*. Philadelphia: Westminister Press, 1976.

Cousins, E., ed. *Process Theology: Basic Writings*. New York: Newman Press, 1971.

DuBois, Ronald L. "Reason in Ethics: A Whiteheadian Perspective." Unpublished dissertation, St. Louis University, 1970.

Feldman, S. "Objectivity, Pluralism and Relativism: A Critique of MacIntyre's Theory of Value." *Southern Journal of Philosophy* 24 (1986): 307–20.

Flanagan, O., and A. O. Rorty. *Identity, Character, and Morality: Essays in Moral Psychology*. Cambridge: MIT University Press, 1990.

Ford, Lewis. "The Origin of Subjectivity." *Modern Schoolman* 62 (1985): 265–76.

———. "Subjectivity in the Making." *Process Studies* 21.1 (1990): 1–24.

Gaita, Raimond. "Virtues, Human Good, and the Unity of a Life." *Inquiry* 26 (1983): 407–24.

George, Robert P. "Moral Particularism, Thomism, and Traditions." *Review of Metaphysics* 42 (1989): 593–605.

Goldman, Alan H. *Moral Knowledge*. New York: Routledge, 1988.

Goodin, Robert, and Andrew Reeve, eds. *Liberal Neutrality*. London: Routledge, 1989.

Hibbs, Thomas S. "MacIntyre, Tradition, and the Christian Philosopher." *Modern Schoolman* 68.3 (1991): 211–23.

Hinmann, Lawrence M. "On the Purity of Our Moral Motives: A Critique of Kant's Account of the Emotions and Acting for the Sake of Duty." *Monist* 66 (1983): 251–67.

Hittinger, Russell. "After MacIntyre: Natural Law Theory, Virtue Ethics, and Eudaimonia." *International Philosophical Quarterly* 29 (1989): 449–61.

Horton, J., and L. Mendus, eds. *After MacIntyre: Critical Perspectives on the Work of Alasdair MacIntyre*. Notre Dame, Ind.: University of Notre Dame Press, 1994.

Janusz, S., and G. Webster. "The Problem of Persons." *Process Studies* 20 (1991): 151–61.

Jones, William R. "Process Theology: Guardian of the Oppressor or Goad to the Oppressed: An Interim Assessment." *Process Studies* 18 (1989): 269–81.

Kant, Immanuel. *Anthropology from a Pragmatic Point of View*. Trans. V. L. Dowdell. Ill.: Southern Illinois University Press, 1978.

——— . *Grounding for the Metaphysics of Morals and Metaphysics of Morals*. In *Immanuel Kant: Ethical Philosophy*. Trans J. W. Ellington. Indianapolis: Hackett, 1983.

LeClerc, Ivor. "The Problem of God in Whitehead's System." *Process Studies* 14 (1995): 301–15.

——— . *Whitehead's Metaphysics: An Introductory Exposition*. Bloomington: Indiana University Press, 1958.

Louden, Robert B. "Kant's Virtue Ethics." *Philosophy* 61 (1986): 473–89.

Lucas, George R. "Agency After Virtue." *International Philosophical Quarterly* 28 (1988): 293–311.

MacIntyre, Alasdair. *After Virtue: A Study in Moral Theory*. Notre Dame, Ind.: University of Notre Dame Press, 1981.

——— . *Against the Self-Image of the Age: Essays in Ideology and Philosophy*. Notre Dame, Ind.: University of Notre Dame Press, 1984.

——— . *First Principles, Final Ends and Contemporary Philosophical Issues*. Milwaukee: Marquette University Press, 1990.

——— . *Three Rival Versions of Moral Enquiry: Encyclopedia, Genealogy, and Tradition*. Notre Dame, Ind.: University of Notre Dame Press, 1990.

——— . *Whose Justice? Which Rationality?* Notre Dame, Ind.: University of Notre Dame Press, 1988.

Mannoia, James. "Is God an Exception to Whitehead's Metaphysics?" In *Process Theology*, ed. Ronald H. Nash. Ada, Mich.: Baker Press, 1984.

Maxwell, Michael P. "A Dialectical Encounter between MacIntyre and Lonergan on the Thomistic Understanding of Rationality." *International Philosophical Quarterly* 33.4 (1993): 385–99.

McCarty, Richard. "Kantian Moral Motivation and the Feeling of Respect." *Journal of the History of Philosophy* 31.3 (1993): 421–35.

Mehl, Peter J. "In the Twilight of Modernity: MacIntyre and Mitchell on Moral Traditions and Their Assessment." *Journal of Religious Ethics* 19.1 (1991): 21–54.

Mesle, Robert C. "'Added on Like Dome and Spire': Weiman's Later Critique of Whitehead." *Process Studies* 20 (1991): 37–53.

Moreland, J. P. "An Enduring Self: The Achilles' Heel of Process Philosophy." *Process Studies* 17 (1988): 193–99.

Mulhall, Stephen, and Adam Swift, eds. *Liberals and Communitarians*. Oxford: Blackwell, 1992.

Neville, Robert C. *Creativity and God: A Challenge to Process Theology*. Albany: State University of New York Press, 1995.

Nobo, Jorge Luis. *Whitehead's Metaphysics of Extension and Solidarity*. Albany: State University of New York Press, 1986.

O'Neill, Onora. "Kant After Virtue." *Inquiry* 26 (1993): 387–406.

Paul, J., and F. Miller Jr. "Communitarian and Liberal Theories of the Good." *Review of Metaphysics* 43.4 (1990): 803–30.

Peden, Creighton W., ed. *God, Values and Empiricism*. Macon, Ga.: Mercer University Press, 1989.

Roque, A. J. "Language Competence and Tradition—Constituted Rationality." *Philosophy and Phenomenological Research* (LI-3) (1991): 611–17.

Schaller, Walter. "Kant on Virtue and Moral Worth." *Southern Journal of Philosophy* 25 (1987): 559–73.

Schindler, David L. "Whitehead's Inability to Affirm a Universe of Value." *Process Studies* 13 (1983): 117–31.

Schneewind, J. B. "MacIntyre and the Indispensability of Tradition." *Philosophy and Phenomenological Research* (LI-3) (1991): 165–68.

——— . "Virtue, Narrative, and Community." *Journal of Philosophy* 79 (1982): 653–63.

Sherburne, D. W. "Decentering Whitehead." *Process Studies* 15 (1986): 83–94.

——— . *A Key to Whitehead's Process and Reality*. New York: Macmillan, 1966.

Thero, Daniel. "Whitehead's God and the Problem of Evil." *Dialogue* 35 (1993): 33–40.

Weisenbeck, J. D. *Alfred North Whitehead's Philosophy of Values*. Waukesha, Wis.: Thomas Press, 1969.

Whitehead, Alfred North. *Adventures of Ideas*. New York: Macmillan, 1933.

——— . *The Aims of Education*. New York: Macmillan, 1929.

——— . *The Function of Reason*. Princeton, N.J.: Princeton University Press, 1929.

——— . *Process and Reality*. Ed. D. R. Griffin and D. W. Sherburne. New York: Free Press, 1978.

——— . *Religion in the Making*. New York: Macmillan, 1926.

——— . *Science and the Modern World*. New York: Macmillan, 1929.

Wolf, George. "Psychological Physiology from the Standpoint of a Physiological Psychologist." *Process Studies* 11 (1981): 274–91.

Index